D0484478

# Trump Talk

DONALD TRUMP IN HIS OWN WORDS

GEORGE BEAHM

Hillsboro Public Library
Hillsboro, OR
A member of Washington County
COOPERATIVE LIBRARY SERVICES

Avon, Massachusetts

Copyright © 2016 by George Beahm.
All rights reserved.
This book, or parts thereof, may not be reproduced in any form without permission from the
publisher; exceptions are made for brief excerpts used in published reviews.

Published by
Adams Media, a division of F+W Media, Inc.
57 Littlefield Street, Avon, MA 02322. U.S.A.
*www.adamsmedia.com*

ISBN 10: 1-4405-9559-3
ISBN 13: 978-1-4405-9559-2
eISBN 10: 1-4405-9560-7
eISBN 13: 978-1-4405-9560-8

Printed in the United States of America.

10   9   8   7   6   5   4   3   2   1

**Library of Congress Cataloging-in-Publication Data**

Beahm, George W., author.
Trump talk / George Beahm.
Avon, Massachusetts: Adams Media, 2016.                    **33614059676584**
Includes index.
LCCN 2015043904 (print) I LCCN 2015045253 (ebook) I ISBN
    9781440595592 (pb) I ISBN 1440595593 (pb) I ISBN 9781440595608 (eISBN) I ISBN
    1440595607 (eISBN)
LCSH: Trump, Donald, 1946---Political and social views. I
    Presidential candidates--United States--Biography. I United
    States--Politics and government--2009-
LCC E901.1.T78 B43 2016 (print) I LCC E901.1.T78 (ebook) I
    DDC 333.33092--dc23
LC record available at *http://lccn.loc.gov/2015043904*

Many of the designations used by manufacturers and sellers to distinguish their products are
claimed as trademarks. Where those designations appear in this book and F+W Media, Inc. was
aware of a trademark claim, the designations have been printed with initial capital letters.

Cover design by Colleen Cunningham.
Cover photography by Gage Skidmore.

*This book is available at quantity discounts for bulk purchases.*
*For information, please call 1-800-289-0963.*

# Contents

*"I have a reputation for being tough, and I'd like to think it's justified. You must be tough when a lot of influential people are saying that your day has come and gone, when your marriage is breaking up, and when business pressures are increasing. Toughness, in the long run, is a major secret of my survival."*

—Donald Trump, *Trump: Surviving at the Top*

# Take Donald Trump Seriously

*"I've told people from the beginning: Never underestimate Donald Trump. He has been very successful for a reason. He knows how to market, and specifically he knows how to market himself, very well. He also understands what the customer wants."*

—Bob Vander Plaats, president of the Family Leader
(*Washington Post*, August 14, 2015)

As with all the candidates running for the presidency of the United States, Donald Trump needs to be taken seriously. After all, he has put his money (he's pledged up to $1 billion), his time, and his reputation on the line. No matter what one thinks of Trump, who in the early stages of the race has towered over his fellow candidates in terms of invaluable media coverage, there can be no dispute that the principal issues he's brought up—immigration, fair trade, foreign policy, jobs, and the federal deficit—stand at the center of every candidate's concerns, regardless of party affiliation.

Win or lose, Trump is in the race. He stands at the center of a political maelstrom inside and outside his party and is on the offensive with a full court press. A Republican win in 2016 potentially means a clean sweep—both houses of Congress and the president will be on the same team. And precisely because the Republicans haven't had one of their own in the Oval Office since George W. Bush (2001–2009), the pressure is on to nominate a winning candidate who can defeat the putative Democratic front-runner, currently Hillary Clinton.

By design, this book is nonpartisan on the subject of Donald Trump, because I want to present a more rounded picture of him. What are his thoughts on his political life, business life, and personal life? By reading his own words, by hand-picking selected quotes from his life from the past forty years that illustrate what today's voters are interested in knowing, we understand how he thinks.

I strove for impartiality precisely because he's a polarizing figure: either people love him or they don't, and their minds are already made up.

I hope that this book will provide food for thought, and show different sides of Trump by putting his life and his run for high office in perspective.

Will Donald trump Hillary? Will both be bushwhacked by Jeb? Or will a dark horse emerge from the shadows?

No one knows, but one thing is for certain: The race is on, the stakes are high, and you can't count anyone out—least of all Donald Trump, a businessman-turned-politician who is anteing up to place the biggest bet of his life.

# Introduction

We have met the enemy, and he is us.

Before the first Republican presidential primary debate, Star Trek-like shields were raised by the Fox News anchors who were concerned about Donald Trump playing a wild card, fearing that he'd ignore the protocol and turn an otherwise formal debate into his own reality TV show. In that event, moderator Bret Baier held a "nuclear option" in reserve: As Stephen Battaglio wrote in the *Los Angeles Times* ("How Fox anchor Bret Baier prepared for the GOP debate and got an instant headline out of Donald Trump," August 9, 2015), in the event Trump went ballistic, they'd tell him, "Mr. Trump, in your business you have rules. You follow rules. We have rules on this stage. We don't want to have to escort you to the elevator outside this boardroom." Baier added: "We're hoping we don't have to use it, [but] we're locked and loaded."

As it turned out, the nuclear option was not needed, but Trump unwittingly created a tempest in a teapot by attacking Megyn Kelly, a Fox News moderator for the debate who asked, ". . . how will you answer the charge from Hillary Clinton, who [is] likely to be the Democratic nominee, that you are part of the war on women?"

# DRAWING BLOOD

Roger Stone, a former political advisor who helped Trump prep for the debate, cautioned him beforehand on how to handle such a question. According to the *Washington Post* ("Growing pains for a sudden front-runner," by Robert Costa and Philip Rucker, August 10, 2015), Stone—who soon thereafter left his position, claiming he resigned, though Trump says he was fired—told him to exercise moderation. "Don't get dragged down by petty attacks, Stone counseled Trump, but begin offering an agenda focused on the economy and hammer home what makes you a singular candidate."

As the newspaper reported, "Trump did not heed the advice. Instead, after briefly flipping through the papers, he decided to wing it—just as he vowed to do."

Instead of explaining, as many think he should have, that he respects women, that he has many women working for him in the Trump Organization, and in key executive positions, and that his random comments shouldn't be taken as representative of the whole, Trump chided Ms. Kelly: "Honestly, Megyn, if you don't like it, I'm sorry. I've been very nice to you, although I could probably maybe not be, based on the way you have treated me. But I wouldn't do that."

But the next day, Trump was out for blood, attacking her online, saying she "had blood coming out of her eyes, blood coming out of her wherever."

Her "wherever" was construed by the media to be a reference to menstrual flow, and Trump suddenly found himself in the middle of a bloodbath, starting with a cancellation as the headlined speaker at Erick Erickson's RedState Gathering in Atlanta scheduled two days later. At his event, Erickson said, "I don't want my daughter in the room with Donald Trump tonight, so he's not invited. If our standard-bearer has to resort to that, then we need a new standard-bearer."

*Time* magazine online (Time.com, August 8, 2015) quoted a spokesman for Trump's campaign who said, "This is just another example of weakness through being politically correct. For all of the people who were looking forward to Mr. Trump coming, we will miss you. Blame Erick Erickson, your weak and pathetic leader. We'll now be doing another campaign stop at another location."

The war of words between Donald Trump and the media at large, and between himself and, indeed, anyone—even with his own party—who in his mind has treated him unfairly, will continue to escalate even as the GOP tries to contain it.

The *Washington Post* ("Trump sparks recoil in GOP," by Philip Rucker and Robert Costa, August 9, 2015) summarized the situation: "Fearful that the billionaire's inflammatory rhetoric has inflicted serious damage to the GOP brand, party leaders hope to pivot away from the Trump sideshow and toward a more serious discussion among a deep field of governors, senators and other candidates." The newspaper continued, "They acknowledge that Trump's unique megaphone and the passion of his supporters make any calculation about his candidacy risky. After all, he has been presumed dead before" after making incendiary comments about fellow Republican and Arizona senator John McCain and fellow candidate Carly Fiorina.

Meanwhile, Democrats—especially front-runner Hillary Clinton—are looking on gleefully, biding their time, expectantly waiting for Donald Trump's campaign to implode.

The big, unanswered question that's keeping everyone on edge is this: In the end, if Trump loses the support of the Republican Party, will he choose the lesser of two evils and simply drop out of the race, instead of siphoning off votes that will help the Democrats win by default if he runs as an independent? It's the central question that has yet to be answered; in the meantime, the world, especially Mexico, is holding its collective breath.

On September 3, Trump signed a pledge, issued by the RNC, to endorse whoever the party picks as its candidate. However, some observers have argued that since the pledge has no legal authority, Trump might decide to jump into the race as a third-party candidate anyway (assuming he is not the nominee), wrecking the party leadership's plans.

So things are in a state of flux; Trump still holds the trump card.

## THE BUSINESS OF AMERICA IS BUSINESS

After building a business empire spanning the globe, Donald Trump is indisputably a hugely successful businessman whose net worth is tallied in the billions. Despite criticisms that he was born into wealth, he disagrees. "The truth is that when I started out in business, I was practically broke. My father didn't give me much money, but what he did was give me a good education and the simple formula for getting wealthy: work hard doing what you love," he wrote in one of his many bestselling books, *Think Big and Kick Ass in Business and Life*.

Trump bristles when reporters say he's not a self-made man; he also bristles, and sometimes threatens lawsuits, when it's reported that he's declared bankruptcy. (He has never *personally* declared bankruptcy, but four of his casinos in Atlantic City have declared *corporate* bankruptcy, which he is quick to point out.)

At heart, Donald Trump is a builder, a street-smart and tough negotiator, and an outspoken critic about how our leaders are running the country.

After several tentative forays in the political arena, he has finally tossed his hat in the ring and announced himself as a presidential candidate for the 2016 race, surprising the Republican Party establishment, which had planned to promote one of their own candidates with extensive legislative experience—traditionally, a state governor or a senator.

As Trump's former advisor Roger Stone told his boss in a memo, quoted in the *Washington Post* (August 10, 2015), he should emphasize his business experience as the panacea for the problems that ail our country. "I'm running because when I look at this field—all perfectly nice people—I know that none of them could ever run one of my companies. They are not entrepreneurs."

## POLL—AND POLE—POSITION

Stone advised Trump to position himself as "a builder, an entrepreneur and a capitalist versus a bunch of politicians who are clearly part of the problem," an important distinction. Many Americans are clearly disenchanted with the prospect of a lot more talk and no action from career politicians—folks the Texans would term "all hat and no cattle."

Tapping deep voter dissatisfaction with politicians, Donald Trump has, to the surprise of the staid GOP, commanded media attention and voter interest, to the point where his popularity in the polls puts him in the lead. (Significantly, the two other non-politicians in the race, Ben Carson and Carly Fiorina, are also doing well.) By doing so, Trump earned a prominent place on stage for the first three Republican presidential debates. Moreover, Trump's presence has electrified the electorate: He's unquestionably the reason Americans tuned in to the debates, when otherwise they'd tune out. As Trump later exclaimed on NBC's *Today* show, "If I wasn't on the show, they would have had 2 million people watching. The other candidates are very lucky because at least people are watching what they're saying as opposed to nobody caring."

The first debate of the campaign in 2011, aired on Fox, drew 3.2 million viewers. But Fox's 2015 debate drew 24 million viewers, making it the most-watched primary debate in television history, and CNN's first debate drew 23 million viewers, setting a new record for the biggest audience in its history—thanks to Donald Trump.

Inquiring minds wanted to know: Who is Donald Trump, and why should he be our next president?

Prior to the debate, *Washington Post* columnist E.J. Dionne Jr. ("Only losers out-Trump Trump," August 3, 2015) concluded: "Trump's supporters have an intuition that something is deeply wrong in their party . . . [T]hey are correct that the party is not delivering what they have a right to expect. Most candidates will play along with the disaffection. Those who try instead to reverse the loss of faith by responding to it constructively will deserve to win the debate."

Who won the debates?

In retrospect, there were no clear winners, including Trump. These are, after all, the first salvos in a long battle that will stretch out for many months, so it's premature to predict a front-runner so early in the game.

The debates were not, as some feared they would be, *The Donald Trump Reality Show*. But speaking from the heart and not from a script, Trump hammered home oft-repeated themes that are the cornerstones of his campaign—issues that he addressed at length in three of his best-selling books, *The America We Deserve* (2000), *Time to Get Tough: Making America #1 Again* (2011) (a second edition of this book was released in September 2015 under the title *Time to Get Tough: Make America Great Again!*), and *Crippled America: How to Make America Great Again* (2015). In all three, he spells out the problems facing the United States, and offers his prescriptions for its cure. In the first book, he writes: "What I would do if elected president would be to appoint myself U.S. trade representative; my lawyers have checked and the president has this authority. I would take personal charge of negotiations with the Japanese, the French, the Germans, and the Saudis. Our trading partners would have to sit across the table from Donald Trump and I guarantee you the rip-off of the United States would end . . . The core of these problems is that we don't know how to negotiate. We don't know how to get what we want out of the people we're sitting across the table from."

In other words, Trump's prescription is to be personally involved and get tough on the issue of foreign trade, because he says we're getting our rumps handed to us by virtually everyone, and needlessly so. It's time, he says, for that to come to a stop.

## ON THE ROAD AGAIN

In future GOP debates, all eyes will be on Trump, to see if he has changed his tune, put a lid on his explosive nature, is prepared with facts and statistics instead of winging it, and appears more presidential; in short, someone who can articulate a plan to save America. If he does that, the other candidates are in for a tough fight.

In *Time* magazine (August 24, 2015), Zeke J. Miller points out that, as far as the GOP is concerned, "prayers for his departure from the race remain unanswered, and the prospect of his sticking around for at least another few months seems high. Trump is the dinner guest who will not leave . . . As long as he stays in the news, owns the debates and floats at the top of the polls, he's ahead."

In other words: hang on to your hats; it's going to be a bumpy flight.

# WHY THIS BOOK?

Back in 1987, when Donald Trump published *Trump: The Art of the Deal*, I bought a copy, read it, and concluded that he was a streetwise, no-nonsense negotiator with big visions to match. In other words, he was not a talker but a doer, and as such, bore watching.

Subsequently, Trump's visions grew bolder, his skyscrapers taller, and he continued to write business books that were candid, refreshing, and educational.

I wondered, after viewing the first Republican presidential debate, if any of his colleagues on the stage had read *any* of his books, which would have been excellent background reading. For any of them to dismiss him out of hand, to not take him seriously, is a mistake. No matter what you think about the man, you can't argue about his success—he's done countless profitable deals over the last four decades that have made him a billionaire; that is an indisputable fact.

As Iowa GOP Chair Jeff Kaufmann stated, in a story for CNN Politics by MJ Lee (October 26, 2015), "I don't think you can find a single Republican in this state that could have predicted that four months ago, Donald Trump would still be in first place (nationally)." He attributes it to a "hunger for an outsider."

# CREDIBLE CANDIDATE—OR NOT?

With all the books by and about him—some authorized, some not—and with all the media coverage he's recently garnered, he's been characterized by his detractors as a "clown" (by Salon.com, and Jack Shafer on Politico.com). Others just as vigorously deny that label: political anchor Errol Louis for

NY1, in the *New York Daily News* (August 4, 2015) asserts that "we should take Trump at his word and treat him like what he is: the leading candidate for the Republican nomination for president. One who has authored two books on how he would govern that contain ideas that fall well within the political mainstream . . . There's no question that Trump the candidate is a media-savvy showman and, at times, a provocateur. But when people compare Trump with the famous nineteenth-century showman and circus owner, P.T. Barnum, they should also remember that Barnum, after making his fortune in amusements, jumped into politics, winning election to the Connecticut legislature and a stint as mayor of Bridgeport. In both jobs, he was considered a vocal and effective reformer."

In other words, don't write Donald Trump off. If you don't take Trump seriously, at least take his bid seriously. At this writing, he appears to be in it for the long haul, and he's opened his wallet. When asked, at a public appearance at the Iowa State Fair (August 15, 2015), if he'd be willing to spend $1 billion of his own money on his campaign, he replied: "I would do that, yeah, if I had to. I make $400 million a year, so what difference does it make?"

Win or lose, though, there's no question that his presence in the race to the White House has shocked and shaken the GOP, and it's transformed the 2016 election into one voters are watching with rapt fascination. Trump speaks plainly, accessibly, to a body politic that for too long has felt disenfranchised, distanced, and disappointed with the same old bumper crop of politicians who toe the party line and, in the end, talk the talk but never walk the walk—Trump says he'll do both.

Trump has obviously touched a raw nerve among Republican voters, bringing up controversial, and to date, insoluble issues that have gotten to the point where they can no longer be ignored. For that reason, he's risen to the top of the polls. Clearly, people are interested in what he has to say.

# "Trump. Make America Great Again!"[1]

*On June 16, 2015, in New York City at Trump Tower,[2] Donald Trump, the founder and head of the Trump Organization, descended an escalator and made his way to a podium. He listened to his daughter Ivanka introduce him to the assemblage. In his hand he held a carefully scripted, four-page speech, prepared by the Donald J. Trump Exploratory Committee. He took to the podium to read it verbatim—the same document his committee had released to the press by e-mail prior to the event, to ensure accuracy in quotes for news stories.*

*The prepared speech was titled: "Trump. Make America Great Again! Donald J. Trump presidential announcement as delivered. Trump Tower, New York City, June 16, 2015."*

*The speech began with a statement of the problem: "Our country is in serious trouble. We are not respected by anyone. We are a laughing stock all over the world. ISIS, China, Mexico are all beating us. Everybody is beating us. Our enemies are getting stronger and we are getting weaker."*

*The speech continued, laying the blame on career politicians who he said "are all talk and no action."*

Saying "I cannot sit back and watch this incompetence any longer," he then offered up himself as the solution. "Ladies and gentlemen, I am officially running for President of the United States."

The statement went on to explain some of the major problems: the growing national debt ("which will soon pass $20 trillion"), unsecured borders, 90 million Americans who have given up looking for work, 45 million Americans on food stamps, and 50 million living in poverty. The statement elaborated on the foreign threat—growing more dangerous daily—that includes Iran and its nuclear weapons, China's expanding military power, Islamic terrorists killing U.S. diplomats in Benghazi, Iran, and ISIS beheading Christians and taking over "vast areas in the Middle East and with it the largest oil reserves in the world."

He proposed the country needs to head in a "bold new direction," that "it is time to get Americans back to work."

His prescriptions: build a wall on the southern border, take care of our veterans, rebuild our military, honor obligations to our seniors, repeal Obamacare, simplify our tax code, stop sending jobs overseas "through bad foreign trade deals," close loopholes on Wall Street, create opportunities for small businesses, invest in our infrastructure, stop Common Core in our schools, stand by Israel, stop Iran from developing nuclear weapons, defeat ISIS, and get tough with the Chinese.

Tough talk.

Clear and concise, Trump's original speech could have been delivered in record time, providing the media with plenty to talk about. This event wasn't the time to provide specifics—that could come later in the campaign—but this speech was the starting point, the firm foundation on which Trump's run for the presidency would be built.

Trump, though, never gave that speech.

*Instead, he used it as an outline to speak extemporaneously. For whatever reasons, he went free form, surprising his campaign staff. A transcript of his impromptu talk quickly appeared online from several media sources, some of whom fact-checked it.*

*Because Trump's impromptu speech is the platform on which he stands as a candidate, I'm reprinting it here, with minor editing—necessary for clarification, and to make it easier to read. I've also added commentary afterward, to provide context.*

*Many of the points in the prepared text would have been welcomed by a disenchanted and frustrated electorate that is looking for a leader who would boldly go where no one has gone before. In general, the main points of Trump's prepared text are in line with those coming from the other Republican candidates seeking their party's nomination.*

It's great to be at Trump Tower. It's great to be in a wonderful city, New York. And it's an honor to have everybody here. This is beyond anybody's expectations. There's [never] been [a] crowd like this.

Our country is in serious trouble. We don't have victories anymore. We used to have victories, but we don't have them. When was the last time anybody saw us beating, let's say, China in a trade deal? They kill us. I beat China all the time.

When did we beat Japan at anything? They send their cars over by the millions, and what do we do? When was the last time you saw a Chevrolet in Tokyo? It doesn't exist, folks. They beat us all the time.

When do we beat Mexico at the border? They're laughing at us, at our stupidity. And now they are beating us economically. They are not our friend, believe me. But they're killing us economically.

The U.S. has become a dumping ground for everybody else's problems.

When Mexico sends its people, they're not sending their best. They're sending people that have lots of problems, and they're bringing those problems to us. They're bringing drugs. They're bringing crime. They're rapists. And some, I assume, are good people.[3]

But I speak to border guards and they tell us what we're getting. And it only makes common sense. They're not sending us the right people. They're not sending [people like you].

It's coming from more than Mexico. It's coming from all over South and [Central] America, and it's coming—probably—from the Middle East. But we don't know. Because we have no protection and we have no competence, we don't know what's happening. And it's got to stop and it's got to stop fast.

Islamic terrorism is eating up large portions of the Middle East. They've become rich. I'm in competition with them. They just built a hotel in Syria. Can you believe this? They built a hotel.[4] When I have to build a hotel, I pay interest. They don't have to pay interest, because they took the oil that, when we left Iraq, I said we should've taken.

So now ISIS has the oil, and what they don't have, Iran has. I will tell you this, and I said it very strongly, years ago, I said—and I love the military, and I want to have the strongest military that we've ever had, and we need it more now than ever—"Don't hit Iraq," because you're going to totally destabilize the Middle East. Iran is going to take over the Middle East, Iran and somebody else will get the oil, and it turned out that Iran is now taking over Iraq. Think of it: Iran is taking over Iraq, and they're taking it over big league.

We spent $2 trillion in Iraq.[5] We lost thousands of lives in Iraq.[6] We have wounded soldiers, whom I love—they're great—all over the place, thousands of wounded soldiers.

And we have nothing. We can't even go there. We have nothing. And every time we give Iraq equipment, the first time a bullet goes off in the air, they leave it.

Last week, I read 2,300 Humvees—these are big vehicles—were left behind for the enemy. Two thousand? You would say maybe two, maybe four? [The Iraqis] ran, and the enemy took 2,300 sophisticated vehicles.[7]

Last quarter, it was just announced, our gross domestic product—a sign of strength, right? But not for us—was below zero. Who ever heard of this? It's never below zero.[8] Our labor participation rate was the worst since 1978. But think of it: GDP below zero, horrible labor participation rate, and our real unemployment is anywhere from 18 to 20 percent. Don't believe the 5.6 percent [figure].[9]

That's right: a lot of people . . . can't get jobs. They can't get jobs because there are no jobs, because China has our jobs, and Mexico has our jobs. They all have our jobs. But the real number is anywhere from 18 to19 percent, and maybe even 21 percent, and nobody talks about it because it's a statistic that's full of nonsense.

Our enemies are getting stronger and stronger by the day and we as a country are getting weaker.

Even our nuclear arsenal doesn't work.[10] They have equipment that's thirty years old, and they don't even know if it works. And I thought it was horrible when it was broadcast on television recently, because boy does that send signals to Putin and all of the other people that look at us, [who] say, "Okay, that is a group of people and that is a nation that truly has no clue. They don't know what they're doing."

We have a disaster called the big lie: Obamacare. Yesterday it came out that costs are going up for people, to 39 percent, 49 percent and even 55 percent.[11] And deductibles are through the roof. You have to get hit by a tractor, literally a tractor, to use it because the deductibles are so high it's virtually useless. It's a disaster.

And remember the $5 billion [Obamacare] website? To this day it doesn't work. A $5 billion website. I have so many websites. I have them all over the place. I hire people, they do a website. It costs me $3.[12]

Well, you need somebody because politicians are all talk, no action. Nothing's going to get done. Believe me, they will not bring us to the promised land. They will not.

As an example, I've been on the circuit making speeches, and I hear my fellow Republicans and they're wonderful people. I like them. They all want me to support them. They come up to my office. I'm meeting with three of them in the next week, and they don't know: Are you running, are you not running, could we have your support, what do we do, how do we do it?

And I like them. I hear their speeches. And they don't talk jobs. They don't talk China. When was the last time you heard "China's killing us"? They're devaluing their currency to a level that you wouldn't believe; it makes it impossible for our companies to compete. Impossible. They're killing us, but you don't hear that from anyone else.

I watch the speeches and they say, "The sun will rise. The moon will set. All sorts of wonderful things will happen." And the people are saying, "What's going on? I just want a job. I don't need the rhetoric, I just want a job." And it's going to get worse because, remember, Obamacare really kicks in in 2016.

Obama is going to be out playing golf. He might even be on one of my courses—I would invite him. I have the best courses in the world. So I say, you know what, if he wants to—I have one right next to the White House, right on the Potomac—if he'd like to play, that's fine. In fact I'd love him to leave early and play. That would be a very good thing. But in 2016 Obamacare kicks in, and it's going to be amazingly destructive.

Doctors are quitting. I have a friend who's a doctor and he said to me the other day: "Donald, I never saw anything like it. I have more accountants than I have nurses. It's a disaster. My patients are beside themselves. They had a plan that was good. They have no plan now."[13]

We have to repeal Obamacare, and it can be replaced with something much better for everybody. Let it be for everybody, but much better and much less expensive for people and for the government. And we can do it.

So I've watched the politicians. I've dealt with them all my life. If you can't make a good deal with a politician, then there's something wrong with you. There's something certainly not very good and that's what we have representing us.

They will never make America great again. They don't even have a chance. They are controlled fully by the lobbyists, by the donors, and by special interests.

Hey, I have lobbyists. I have to tell you, I have lobbyists that can produce anything for me. They're great. But you know what? It won't happen. It won't happen because we have to stop doing things for some people, but it's destroying this country. We have to stop and it has to stop now.

Our country needs a truly great leader now. We need a leader that wrote *The Art of the Deal*.[14] We need a leader that can bring back our jobs, our manufacturing, our military, and can take care of our vets, [who] have been abandoned. And we also need a cheerleader.

When President Obama was elected, I said, "Well, the one thing I think he'll do well—I think he'll be a great cheerleader for the country. I think he'd be a great spirit." He was vibrant. He was young. I really thought he would be a great cheerleader.

It's true that he's not a leader. You're right about that. But he wasn't a cheerleader. He's actually been a negative force. He wasn't a cheerleader; he was the opposite.

We need somebody that can take the brand of the United States and make it great again. It's not great.

We need somebody that literally will take this country and make it great again. We can do that.

And, I will tell you, I love my life. I have a wonderful family. They're saying, "Dad, you're going to do something that's so tough." You know, all of my life I've heard that a truly successful person—a really successful person, and even modestly successful—cannot run for public office. Just can't happen. And yet, that's the kind of mindset that you need to make this country great again.

So, ladies and gentlemen, I am officially running for president of the United States and we are going to make our country great again. It can happen. Our country has tremendous potential. We have tremendous potential.

We have people that aren't working. We have people that have no incentive to work. But they're going to have incentive to work, because the greatest social program is a job. And they'll be proud, and they'll love it, and they'll make much more money than they would have ever made. And they'll be doing so well, and we're going to be thriving as a country. It can happen.

I will be the greatest jobs president that God ever created, I tell you that. I'll bring back our jobs from China, from Mexico, from Japan, from so many places. I'll bring back our jobs, and I'll bring back our money.

Right now—think of this—we owe China $1.3 trillion.[15] We owe Japan more than that. So they come in, they take our jobs, they take our money, and then they loan us back the money and we pay them in interest. And then the dollar goes up, so their deal's even better.

How stupid are our leaders? How stupid are these politicians to allow this to happen?

I'm going to tell you a couple of stories about trade, because I'm totally against the trade bill for a number of reasons.

Number one: the people negotiating it don't have a clue. Our president doesn't have a clue. He's a bad negotiator. He's the one that did Bergdahl.[16] We get Bergdahl; they get five killer terrorists that everybody wanted over there. We get a no-good traitor and they get the five people that they wanted for years. And those people are now back on the battlefield trying to kill us. That's the negotiator we have.

Take a look at the deal he's making with Iran. He makes that deal, Israel maybe won't exist very long. It's a disaster and we have to protect Israel.

I'm a free trader, but the problem with free trade is, you need really talented people to negotiate for you. If you don't have talented people, if you don't have great leadership, if you don't have people that know business—not just a political hack that got the job because he made a contribution to a campaign, which is the way all jobs just about are gotten—free trade is terrible.

Free trade can be wonderful if you have smart people. But we have people that are stupid. We have people that aren't smart, and we have people that are controlled by special interests, and it's just not going to work.

China comes over and they dump all their stuff. I buy it because, frankly, I have an obligation to buy it, because they devalue their currency so brilliantly. They just did it recently and nobody thought they could do it again; but with all our problems with Russia, and with everything, they got away with it again. And it's impossible for our people here to compete. So here's a couple of stories. Happened recently. A friend of mine is a great manufacturer. Calls me up a few weeks ago, he's very upset.

I said, "What's your problem?"

He said, "You know, I make a great product."

I said, "I know, because I buy the product."

He said, "I can't get it into China. They won't accept it. I sent a boat over and they actually sent it back. They talked about environmental, they talked about all sorts of crap that had nothing to do with it."

I said, "Oh, wait a minute, that's terrible. Did anyone know this?"

He said, "They do it all the time with other people."

I said, "They send it back?"

He said, "Yeah, so I finally got it over there, and they charged me a big tariff."

"They're not supposed to be doing that. That's a terrible story, I hate to hear it."

People say, "Oh, you don't like China." No, I love them, but their leaders are much smarter than our leaders. And we can't sustain ourselves with that.

Now, they do charge you tariffs when we send trucks and other things over there. Ask Boeing. They wanted all their patents and secrets before they agreed to buy planes from Boeing.

Hey, I'm not saying they're stupid. I like China. I just sold an apartment for $15 million to somebody from China. Am I supposed to dislike them?

I own a big chunk of the Bank of America building at 1290 Avenue of Americas that I got from China. Very valuable. I love China.

The biggest bank in the world is from China. You know where their United States headquarters is located? In this building, in Trump Tower.

There's too much [disparity]. It's like . . . take the New England Patriots and Tom Brady and have them play your high school football team. That's the difference between China's leaders and our leaders.

They are ripping us. We are rebuilding China. We are rebuilding many countries.

China's got roads, bridges, schools. You never saw anything like it. They have bridges that make the George Washington Bridge look like small potatoes. And they're all over the place. We have all the cards, but we don't know how to use them. We don't even know that we have the cards, because our leaders don't understand the game.

We would turn off that spigot by charging them tax until they behave properly.

Now they're building a military island in the middle of the South China Sea—a military island.[17] Now, our country could never do that because we'd have to get environmental clearance and the environmentalists wouldn't let our country. We would never be able to build in an ocean.

They built it in about one year, this massive military port. They're building up their military to a point that is very scary.

You have a problem with ISIS; you have a bigger problem with China.

And in my opinion, the new China, believe it or not, in terms of trade is Mexico.

But I have another [story], Ford. So Mexico takes a car company that was going to build in Tennessee and rips it out.

Everybody thought the deal was dead, reported in the *Wall Street Journal* recently. Everybody said that it was a done deal. It's going in, and that's going to be it, going into Tennessee—great state, great people. All of a sudden, at the last moment, this big car manufacturer announces they're not going to Tennessee—they're going to spend their billion dollars in Mexico instead. Not good.

Ford announces a few weeks ago that they're going to build a $2.5 billion car and truck and parts manufacturing plant in Mexico. It's going to be one of the largest in the world.[18]

I know the smartest negotiators in the world. I know the good ones, the bad ones, the overrated ones.

You've got a lot that are overrated. They get good stories because the newspapers get buffaloed. But they're not good. But I know the best negotiators in the world and I'd put them one for each country. Believe me folks, we will do very, very well.

But I wouldn't even waste my time with this one. I would call up the head of Ford, whom I know. If I was president, I'd say, "Congratulations! I understand that you're building a $2.5 billion factory in Mexico and that you're going to take your cars and sell them to the United States. Zero tax— just across the board."

And you say to yourself, "How does that help us? Where is that good?" It's not.

I'd say, "Congratulations, that's the good news. Let me give you the bad news: We're going to charge you a 35 percent tax for every car, and every truck and every part manufactured in this plant that comes across the border. And that tax is going to be paid simultaneously with the transaction, and that's it."

If it's not me in the position, if it's one of these politicians that we're running against, here's what's going to happen. They're not so stupid. They know it's not a good thing. And they may even be upset by it, but then they're going to get a call from their donors, or probably from the lobbyists for Ford, and say, "You can't do that to Ford, because Ford takes care of me, and I take care of you, and you can't do that to Ford."

And you know what? No problem. They're going to build in Mexico, and they're going to take away thousands of jobs. That's very bad for us. So under President Trump, here's what would happen: The head of Ford will call me back, I would say, within an hour after I told him the bad news, but it could be he'd want to be cool and he'll wait until the next day.

And he'll say, "Please, please, please." He'll beg for a little while, and I'll say, "Sorry, no interest."

Then he'll call all sorts of political people, and I'll say, "Sorry fellas, no interest." Because I don't need anybody's money. It's nice. I'm using my own money [for my campaign]. I'm not using lobbyists. I'm not using donors. I don't care. I'm really rich. And by the way, I'm not even saying that to brag. That's the kind of mindset, the kind of thinking you need for this country. Because we've got to make the country rich.

It sounds crass. Somebody said, "Oh, that's crass." It's not crass. We've got $18 trillion in debt.[19] We've got nothing but problems. We've got a military that needs equipment all over the place. We've got nuclear weapons that are obsolete. We've got nothing. We've got Social Security that's going to be destroyed if somebody like me doesn't bring money into the country. All these other people want to cut the hell out of it. I'm not going to cut it at all. I'm going to bring money in, and we're going to save it.

But here is what's going to happen. After I'm called by thirty friends of mine who contributed to different campaigns, after I'm called by all of the special interests, by the donors, and by the lobbyists, they have zero chance at convincing me. Zero.

I'll get a call the next day from the head of Ford. He'll say, "Please reconsider."

I'll say, "No."

He'll say, "Mr. President, we've decided to move the plant back to the United States. We're not going to build it in Mexico."

That's it. They'll have no choice. There are hundreds of things like that.

I'll give you another example: Saudi Arabia. They make a billion dollars a day. I love the Saudis. Many are in this building. Whenever they have problems, we send over the ships. We're going to protect [them for free].[20]

What are we doing? They got nothing but money. If the right person asked them, they'd pay a fortune. They wouldn't be there except for us.

Look at the border with Yemen.[21] You remember Obama [said] a year ago, Yemen was a great victory. Two weeks later the place was blown up.

And they kept our equipment. They always keep our equipment. We ought to send used equipment, right? They always keep our equipment, we ought to send some real junk, our surplus. We're always losing this gorgeous, brand-new stuff.

But look at that border with Saudi Arabia. Do you really think that these people are interested in Yemen? Saudi Arabia without us is gone.

And I'm the one that made all of the right predictions about Iraq. Look at Jeb Bush. It took him five days to answer the question on Iraq. He couldn't answer the question. He didn't know.[22]

I said, "Is he intelligent?" And then I looked at [Marco] Rubio. He was unable to answer the question. He didn't know.

How are these people going to lead us? How are we going to go back and make it great again? We can't. They don't have a clue. They can't lead us. They can't. They can't even answer simple questions.

Saudi Arabia is in big, big trouble. Now, thanks to fracking and other things, the oil is all over the place. And I used to say it, there are ships at sea—and this was during the worst crisis—that were loaded up with oil. And the cartel kept the prices up because, again, they were smarter than our leaders. There is so much wealth out there that we can make our country so rich again and, therefore, make it great again.

We need money. We're dying. We have to do it, and we need the right people, so Ford will come back; they'll all come back. And I will say this: This is going to be an election, in my opinion, that's based on competence.

Somebody said to me the other day, a very nice reporter, "But Mr. Trump, you're not a nice person." But actually, I am. I think I'm a nice person. Does my family like me? I think so. Look at my family. I'm proud of my family, by the way. Speaking of my family—Melania, Barron, Kai, Donny, Dunn, Vanessa, Tiffany, Jarrett, Laura, and Eric—Ivanka did a great job [introducing me today]. I'm very proud of my family. They're a great family.

So the reporter said to me the other day, "But Mr. Trump, you're not a nice person. How can you get people to vote for you?"

I said, "I don't know. I think that, number one, I am a nice person. I give a lot of money away to charities and other things." I think I'm actually a very nice person, but I said, "This is going to be an election that's based off competence. Because people are tired of these nice people and they're tired of being ripped off by everybody in the world, and they're tired of spending more money on education than any nation in the world per capita."[23]

And we're twenty-sixth in the world. Twenty-five countries are better than us at education, and some of them are like third-world countries. But we're becoming a third-world country because of our infrastructure, our airports, our roads, everything. So one of the things I did, and I said, "You know what I'll do? I'll do it." And a lot of people said, "He'll never run. Number one, he won't want to give up his lifestyle." They're right about that, but I'm doing it.

Number two, I'm a private company, so nobody knows what I'm worth. And the one thing is, when you run, you have to announce and certify [your] net worth to all sorts of governmental authorities. So I said, "That's okay, I'm proud of my net worth." I've done an amazing job.

I started off in a small office with my father in Brooklyn and Queens. He was a great negotiator. I learned so much just sitting as his feet playing with blocks, listening to him negotiate with subcontractors. But I learned a lot. "Donald, don't go into Manhattan. That's the big leagues. We don't know anything about that. Don't do it."

But I said, "Dad, I gotta go into Manhattan. I gotta build those buildings. I've got to do it, Dad, I've got to do it." And after four or five years in Brooklyn, I ventured into Manhattan and did a lot of great deals: the Grand Hyatt hotel; I was [also] responsible for the convention center on the West Side.

I did a lot of great deals and I did them early and young, and now I'm building all over the world. And I love what I'm doing. But a lot of the pundits on television all said, "Well, Donald will never run, and one of the main reasons is, he's private, and he's probably not as successful as everybody thinks."

So I said to myself, "You know, nobody's ever going to know unless I run because I'm really proud of my success, I really am." I've employed tens of thousands of people over my lifetime. That means medical, that means education, that means everything.[24]

So a large accounting firm and my accountants have been working for months, because I'm big and complex, and they put together a financial statement. It's a summary, but everything will be filed eventually with the government. And we don't need extensions or anything, we'll be filing it right on time. And it was even reported incorrectly yesterday, because they said [I] had assets of $9 billion.

I said, "No, that is the wrong number. That's the wrong number, not assets."

So they put this together, and before I say it, I have to say this: I made it the old-fashioned way. It's real estate. It's labor and it's union—good and some bad—and lots of people that aren't unions, and it's all over the place and building all over the world. And I have assets—big accounting firm, one of the most highly respected—$9.24 billion. And I have liabilities of about $500 million, that's long-term debt [at] very low interest rates.

In fact, one of the big banks came to me, said, "Donald, you don't have enough borrowing. Can we loan you $4 billion?" I said, "I don't need it. I don't want it. I've been there. I don't want it."

But in two seconds they give me whatever I wanted. So I have a total net worth, and now with the increase, it'll be well over $10 billion. But here, a total net worth—not assets—of $8,737,540,000.

I'm not doing that to brag, because you know what? I don't have to brag. I don't have to, believe it or not. I'm doing that to say that that's the kind of thinking our country needs. We need that thinking. We have the opposite thinking.

We have losers. We have people that don't have it. We have people that are morally corrupt. We have people that are selling this country down the drain.

So I put together this statement, and the only reason I'm telling you about it today is because we really do have to get going, because if we have another three or four years—you know, we're at $8 trillion now—we're soon going to be at $20 trillion.

According to the economists, who I'm not a big believer in, but nevertheless, this is what they're saying, that we're very close [to] the point of no return—$24 trillion.[25] We will be there soon. That's when we become Greece. That's when we become a country that's unsalvageable. And we're gonna be there very soon. We're gonna be there very soon.

So, just to sum up, I would do various things very quickly.

I would repeal and replace the big lie, Obamacare.

I would build a great wall—and nobody builds walls better than me, believe me, and I'll build them very inexpensively—on our southern border. And I will have Mexico pay for that wall. Mark my words.

Nobody would be tougher on ISIS than Donald Trump. Nobody.

I will find within our military [our] General Patton or General MacArthur. I will find the guy that's going to take that military and make it really work. Nobody will be pushing us around.

I will stop Iran from getting nuclear weapons. And we won't be using a man like Secretary Kerry that has absolutely no concept of negotiation, who's making a horrible and laughable deal, who's just being tapped along as they make weapons right now, and then goes into a bicycle race at seventy-two years old, and falls and breaks his leg. I won't be doing that. And I promise I will never be in a bicycle race. That I can tell you.[26]

I will immediately terminate President Obama's illegal executive order on immigration.[27]

I will fully support and back up the Second Amendment.

Through stupidity, in a very hardcore prison, two vicious murderers escaped, and nobody knows where they are.[28] And a woman up in the prison area was on television this morning, and she said, "You know, Mr. Trump, I always was against guns. I didn't want guns. And now since this happened, my husband and I are finally in agreement, because he wanted the guns. We now have a gun on every table. We're ready to start shooting."

I said, "Very interesting."

So protect the Second Amendment.

End Common Core.[29] Common Core is a disaster. Education has to be local. Bush is totally in favor of Common Core.

I don't see how he can possibly get the nomination. He's weak on immigration. He's in favor of Common Core. How the hell can you vote for this guy? You just can't do it.

Rebuild the country's infrastructure. Nobody can do that like me. Believe me, it will be done on time, on budget, way below cost, way below what anyone ever thought.

I look at the roads being built all over the country, and I say I can build those things for one-third. What they do is unbelievable. How bad?

We're building on Pennsylvania Avenue, the Old Post Office, and converting it into one of the world's great hotels.[30] It's gonna be the best hotel in Washington, D.C. We got it from the General Services Administration in Washington. The Obama administration. It was the most highly sought after—or one of them—project in the history of General Services.

We got it. People were shocked [that] Trump got it. Well, I got it for two reasons. Number one, we're really good. Number two, we had a really good plan. And I'll add in the third: We had a great financial statement. Because the General Services, who are terrific people, by the way, and talented people, they wanted to do a great job. And they wanted to make sure it got built.

So we have to rebuild our infrastructure, our bridges, our roadways, our airports.

You come into LaGuardia Airport, and it's like we're in a third-world country. You look at the patches and the forty-year-old floor.[31]

And I come in from China, come in from Qatar, come in from different places, and they have the most incredible airports in the world. You come back to this country and you have LAX, a disaster. You have all of these disastrous airports. We have to rebuild our infrastructure.

Save Medicare, Medicaid, and Social Security without cuts. We have to do it.

Get rid of the fraud. Get rid of the waste and abuse, but save it. People have been paying it for years. And now many of these candidates want to cut it. You save it by making the United States, by making us rich again, by taking back all of the money that's being lost.

Renegotiate our foreign trade deals.

Reduce our $18 trillion in debt, because, believe me, we're in a bubble. We have artificially low interest rates. We have a stock market that, frankly, has been good to me, but I still hate to see what's happening. We have a stock market that is so bloated. Be careful of a bubble because what you've seen in the past might be small potatoes compared to what happens [in the future]. So be very, very careful.

And strengthen our military and take care of our vets. So, so important.

Sadly, the American dream is dead, but if I get elected president I will bring it back bigger and better and stronger than ever before, and we will make America great again.

Thank you very much.

# ENDNOTES

[1]**Trump's campaign slogan:** Recalling Ronald Reagan's slogan, Trump's 2016 presidential campaign slogan is "Make America Great Again!" He registered it as a trademark (filed November 19, 2012, registered July 14, 2015, registration number 4773272), thus preventing other politicians from using it. As for his platform, the blueprint for his "Make American Great Again!" campaign can be found in three books: *The America We Deserve* (Renaissance Books, 2000), *Time to Get Tough: Making America #1 Again* (Regnery Publishing, 2011), and *Crippled America: How to Make America Great Again* (Threshold Editions, November 2015).

[2]**Trump Tower:** Trump Tower was completed in 1983. Located between East 56th and 57th streets in New York City, the tower rises 68 stories: floors 1–26 are luxury offices, 27 and 28 are Trump's offices, and floors 30–68 are residential condos with a private entrance. Trump Tower includes a grill, a café, a bar, a gift shop, and a retail store. (Source: *www.TrumpTowerNY.com*).

In *Trump: The Art of the Deal* (Random House, 1987), "Trump Tower: The Tiffany Location," he writes: "Ultimately, Trump Tower became much more than just another good deal. I work in it, I live in it, and I have a very special feeling about it. And it's because I have such a personal attachment that I ended up buying out my partner, Equitable, in 1986."

Trump Tower is now 100 percent owned by the man whose name is emblazoned in large, gold, capital letters above its main entrance.

[3]**Mexican immigration:** In George Will's *Washington Post* column, August 23, 2015, quoting Trump ("They've got to go"), he explains: "'They,' the approximately 11.3 million illegal immigrants . . . have these attributes: Eighty-eight percent have been here at least five years. Of the 62 percent who have been here at least 10 years, about 45 percent own their own homes. About half have children who were born here and hence are citizens. Dara Lind of Vox reports that at least 4.5 million children who are citizens have at least one parent who is an illegal immigrant." But the *Washington Post* columnist satirically points out that, for Trump, where there's a will, there's a way: "But Trump wants America to think big. The big costs, in decades and dollars (hundreds of billions), of Trump's project could be reduced if, say, the targets were required to sew yellow patches on their closing to advertise their coming expulsion. There is precedent."

[4]**Terrorist hotel:** According to PolitiFact.com ("Donald Trump: ISIS built a hotel in Syria," by Lauren Carroll, June 16, 2015), "The grain of truth here is that the Islamic State has taken over a luxury hotel. But they didn't build it. And it's not in Syria. And it doesn't really operate like a normal hotel. We couldn't find any evidence that the Islamic State is running any sort of hotel in Syria. We tried to get in touch with a Trump spokesperson and didn't hear back. However, this May, the Islamic State reopened a five-star hotel in Mosul that shut down when the terrorist group took over the city, one of the largest in Iraq . . . So the Islamic State didn't build the Ninawa International Hotel; they just occupied it. Also, it's not really open for business. According to news reports, the Islamic State is using the hotel's 262 rooms to house the group's commanding officers, and they might use it as a wedding venue for the group's members."

[5]**Cost of the Iraq War:** According to Reuters ("Iraq war costs U.S. more than $2 trillion: study," by Daniel Trotta, March 14, 2013), "The U.S. war in Iraq has cost $1.7 trillion with an additional $490 billion in benefits owed to war veterans, expenses that could grow to more than $6 trillion over the next four decades counting interest, a study released on Thursday said."

[6]**U.S. casualties sustained in the wars in Iraq and Afghanistan:** In a report, ("US and Coalition Casualties in Iraq and Afghanistan," by Catherine Lutz of the Watson Institute for International Studies, Brown University, February 21, 2013), Lutz states, "The US military has carefully counted its uniformed dead in the wars in Iraq and Afghanistan. As of February 14, 2013, that number totaled 6,656."

[7]**ISIS captures over $1 billion worth of abandoned Humvees:** A British newspaper, the *Guardian*, reported on May 31, 2015, in a story titled "Isis captured 2,300 Humvee armored vehicles from Iraqi forces in Mosul," that "Iraq security forces lost 2,300 Humvee armored vehicles when the Islamic State jihadist group overran the northern city of Mosul, the prime minister Haider al-Abadi said on Sunday." The paper notes that the exact price of the Humvees isn't possible because it "varies depending on how they are armored and equipped . . ." It notes that the U.S. State Department "approved a possible sale to Iraq of 1,000 Humvees with increased armor, machine-guns, grenade launchers, other gear and support, which was estimated to cost $579 million." Based on that, 2,300 similarly equipped/supported Humvees would cost $579,000 each, giving a loss of $1.33 billion in state-of-the-art U.S. vehicles now used by the enemy when the Iraqis cut and run. (The newspaper also noted that "the militants gained ample arms,

ammunition and other equipment when multiple Iraqi divisions fell apart in the country's north, abandoning gear and shedding uniforms in their haste to flee. ISIS has used captured Humvees, which were provided to Iraq by the United States, in subsequent fighting, rigging some with explosives for suicide bombings."

[8]**U.S. gross domestic product:** The Bureau of Economic Analysis (*www.bea.gov/ newsreleases/national/gdp/2015/gdp2q15_adv.htm*) released a statement, July 30, 2015, that "Real gross domestic product—the value of the production of goods and services in the United States, adjusted for price changes—increased at an annual rate of 2.3 percent in the second quarter of 2015, according to the 'advance' estimate released by the Bureau of Economic Analysis. In the first quarter, real GDP increased 0.6 percent (revised)."

[9]**Unemployment:** NPR ("Unemployment Rate Steady as Economy Adds 215,000 Jobs," by Scott Neuman, August 7, 2015), states that "The U.S. economy added 215,000 jobs last month, just shy of the number forecast by economists. The unemployment rate remained unchanged at 5.3 percent." PolitiFact.com (June 16, 2015) researched Trump's claim (Louis Jacobson, researcher; edited by Angie Drobnic Holan), and disagreed with his assessment. Trump is incorporating figures for under-employment, which raises the unemployment number higher. However, according to PolitiFact, "Trump is off-base even if you give him the maximum benefit of the doubt. The highest official government statistic for under-employment is 10.8 percent—roughly half as high as Trump says. And if you make a quick and dirty attempt to expand the scope of this measure to include other Americans left uncounted in the standard statistics, there's no plausible way to get it past 16 percent—and even that's stretching it. That's well below the range Trump cited, so we rate the claim false."

[10]**Our aging nuclear arsenal:** The *Los Angeles Times* ("Aging nuclear arsenal grows ever more costly," by Ralph Vartabedian and W.J. Hennigan, November 8, 2014), explains that "The nation's nuclear weapons stockpile has shrunk by 85% since its Cold War peak half a century ago, but the Energy Department is spending nine times more on each weapon that remains. The nuclear arsenal will cost $8.3 billion this fiscal year, up 30% over the last decade." The newspaper quotes Roger Logan ("a senior nuclear scientist who retired in 2007 from Lawrence Livermore National Laboratory"): "We are not getting enough for what we are spending, and we are spending more than what we need. The whole system has failed us." The paper also quotes a retired four-star Air Force

general, and former Air Force chief of staff, Norton A. Schwartz: "If modernization isn't done properly, the perception of U.S. strength is at risk—and by extension our national security is at risk."

[11]**Obamacare rate increases:** In *Forbes* ("Why Are the 2016 Obamacare Rate Increases So Large?," by Robert Laszewski [president of Health Policy and Strategy Associates LLC, in Washington, D.C.], June 10, 2015), Laszewski explains, "Instead of moderate increases for one more year, the big rate increases have begun." Texas Blue Cross is asking "only" for a 20 percent rate increase; CareFirst Blue Cross of Maryland, 34 percent on its PPO plan, and 26.7 percent for its HMO plan; in Oregon, Moda is asking for a 25.6 percent increase, and LifeWise a 38.5 percent increase; Blue Cross Blue Shield of Tennessee, a 36.3 percent increase, and Humana a 15.8 percent increase; in Georgia, Humana is asking for individual plans increasing to 19.44 percent; in Kansas, an increase "as much as 38 percent"; and in Pennsylvania, Highmark is asking 39.65 percent, and Geisinger HMO 58.4 percent.

[12]**Cost of erecting Obamacare website:** Bloomberg.com states: "The federal government's Obamacare enrollment system has cost about $2.1 billion so far, according to a Bloomberg Government analysis of contracts related to the project." ("Obamacare Website Costs Exceed $2 Billion, Study Finds," by Alex Wayne, September 24, 2014.) It should be noted that the website does, in fact, work.

[13]**Physicians rate Obamacare:** The Physicians Foundation's survey of 20,000 doctors indicated that "46 percent gave Obamacare a D or F grade, while 25 percent gave it an A or B grade." ("Is It True? Do Doctors Really Loathe Obamacare?," by David Mills, Healthline.com, April 14, 2015.)

[14]***The Art of the Deal:*** His first bestselling book, *Trump: The Art of the Deal* was on the *New York Times* bestseller list for fifty-one weeks. Published by Random House as a trade hardback in 1987, *Publishers Weekly* said it was a "boastful, boyishly disarming, thoroughly engaging personal history [that] offers an inside look of financing, development and construction in big-time New York real estate." *PW* notes that it had a first printing of 135,000 copies. *Library Journal* wrote, "This is a fascinating book because it is incredible. At the age of 41, Trump, the son of a Queens, New York, developer of moderate-income apartment houses, presides over a vast real estate empire with assets in the billions. Trump's world is composed of an endless series of deals and

ventures, most of them monumentally successful from his point of view . . . Trump seems to be a clever entrepreneur and exhibitionist."

[15]**Foreign debt:** In a story on About.com ("How Much U.S. Debt Does China Really Own?," by Tom Murse, not dated), it's stated that "Foreign governments hold about 46 percent of all U.S. debt held by the public, more than $4.5 trillion. The largest foreign holder of U.S. debt is China, which owns more than about $1.2 trillion in bills, notes and bonds, according to the Treasury . . . Other large foreign holders of U.S. debt include Japan, which owns $912 billion; the United Kingdom, which owns $347 billion; Brazil, which holds $211 billion; Taiwan, which holds $153 billion; and Hong Kong, which owns $122 billion." (These are 2011 figures.)

[16]**Bowe Bergdahl:** Eric Schmitt and Charlie Savage of the *New York Times* ("Bowe Bergdahl, American Soldier, Freed by Taliban in Prisoner Trade," May 31, 2014) wrote that "The lone American prisoner of war from the Afghan conflict, captured by insurgents nearly five years ago, has been released to American forces in exchange for five Taliban detainees held at Guantanamo Bay, Cuba, Obama administration officials said Saturday . . . The five Taliban detainees at Guantanamo, including two senior militant commanders said to be linked to operations that killed American and allied troops as well as implicated in murdering thousands of Shiites in Afghanistan, were flown from Cuba . . ."

[17]**China's military island:** "New [satellite] images taken just this week show China building what look like military bases on reclaimed land in the South China Sea, a development likely to add to concerns in the United States and among its Asian neighbors . . . On June 16, China's Foreign Ministry announced 'that infrastructure will mainly be for civilian purposes but acknowledges it will also be used for 'military defense.'" ("See China's rapid island-building strategy in action," by Simon Denyer, *Washington Post,* July 1, 2015.)

In a story online from CNN by Jim Sciutto and Katie Hunt ("China says it warned and tracked U.S. warship in South China Sea," October 27, 2015), China's Foreign Ministry spokesman Lu Kang said, "If any country thinks that, through some gimmicks, they will be able to interfere with or even prevent China from engaging in reasonable, legitimate and legal activities in its own territories, I want to suggest those countries give up such fantasy. In fact, if relevant parties insist on creating tensions in the region and making trouble out of nothing, it may force China to draw the conclusion that we need to strengthen and hasten the buildup of our relevant capabilities. I advise the U.S. not to create such a self-fulfilling prophecy."

[18]**Ford Motor Company:** "Ford Motor Co. said on Friday it will spend $2.5 billion to build a new generation of fuel-efficient engines and transmissions in Mexico, creating 3,800 jobs. The United Auto Workers union, in response, said putting jobs in Mexico rather than the United States will be a major issue at its upcoming U.S. labor talks with Ford, General Motors Co. and Fiat Chrysler Automobiles." ("Ford to spend $2.5 billion on plants in Mexico, angering UAW," by Luis Rojas and Bernie Woodall, Reuters.com, April 17, 2015.)

[19]**U.S. debt:** "If Washington doesn't act soon, will the debt become an unmanageable burden? I believe the answer to this question lies somewhere between 'absolutely' and 'very likely' . . . You cannot circumvent the laws of economics. If we continue to accumulate debt, if we ignore the warning signs, if our officials maintain the status quo, there will be consequences. I only hope America realizes it before it's too late." ("How Much Each Taxpayer Owes Toward the Federal Debt," by Alan Joel, TaxPolitix.com, April 26, 2015.)

[20]**Saudi oil:** "Saudi Arabia has secretly increased its oil production to 9.8m barrels per day, its highest level of output since last October, in a push to win back market share in its oil price war with US shale drillers. Speaking at a conference in the kingdom, Khalid-al-Falih, chief executive of Saudi Aramco—the country's state-run oil company—said: 'Supply and demand and the rules of economics will govern. It will take time for the current glut to be removed.'" ("Saudi Arabia increases oil output to crush US shale frackers," by Andrew Critchlow, Telegraph.co.uk, January 27, 2015.)

[21]**Yemen:** CBS News ("Yemen crisis prompts U.S. withdrawal, emergency U.N. meeting," March 22, 2015) reported that "The U.N. Security Council will hold an emergency meeting Sunday to discuss the deteriorating situation in Yemen . . . The overall fear is that Yemen—the Arab world's most impoverished country, united only in the 1990s—could topple toward another civil war. The possible presence of an ISIS-linked group complicates the situation, since al-Qaeda and the extremists who hold a third of Iraq and Syria are already rivals."

[22]**Jeb Bush on the Iraq War:** In the first Republican presidential debate, when asked by Megyn Kelly about the Iraq War, former Florida governor Jeb Bush said, "Knowing what we know now, with faulty intelligence, and not having security be the first priority when we invaded, it was a mistake. I wouldn't have gone in . . ." (Republican presidential debate, airing on Fox News cable channel, August 6, 2015.)

[23]**U.S. student education expenditures:** "The United States spends more than other developed nations on its students' education each year . . . Despite the spending, U.S. students still trail their rivals on international tests . . . The United States spent more than $11,000 per elementary student in 2010 and more than $12,000 per high school student. When researchers factored in the cost for programs after high school education such as college or vocational training, the United States spent $15,171 on each young person in the system—more than any other nation covered in the report." ("U.S. education spending tops global list, study shows," CBSNews.com, June 25, 2013, summarizing from OECD (2013), *Education at a Glance 2013: OECD Indicators*, OECD Publishing.)

In mathematics, the U.S. ranks thirty-fifth out of sixty-four countries; and in science, twenty-seventh out of sixty-four countries worldwide on the 2012 Program for International Student Assessment. ("U.S. students improving—slowly—in math and science, but still lagging internationally," by Drew DeSilver, PewResearch.org, February 2, 2015.)

[24]**Employment at the Trump Organization:** CNN reports that "The Trump Organization employs 22,000 people. But Trump also runs a number of other companies that employ fewer than 500, meaning that—under the federal government's definition—he qualifies as a small business." ("Fact Check: Is Donald Trump a small business?," by the CNN Wire Staff, CNNPolitics.com, October 5, 2012.)

[25]**Burgeoning national debt:** "Last week, the national debt surpassed $18 trillion. That's $124,000 for each American household or $56,378 per individual. It took the country 205 years to accumulate its first trillion dollars of debt in 1981, but has only taken us 403 days to accumulate our most recent trillion . . . Last year, the U.S. spent $430 billion on interest payments alone . . . Say interest rates rise to 5 percent . . . That means we will owe nearly $1 trillion a year in interest alone. That's about two-thirds of what the federal government brings in each year in total income tax revenue!" ("The U.S. is Now $18 Trillion in Debt," InformationStation.org, December 5, 2014.)

[26]**Bicyclist John Kerry:** John Kerry was not in a bicycle race. As the British newspaper the *Guardian* explained, he "broke his leg in [a] bike crash near Scionzier in France on Sunday, apparently after hitting a curb." ("John Kerry breaks leg in cycling accident . . . ," by staffers, TheGuardian.com, May 31, 2015.)

[27]**Obama's immigration policy:** For the Debate Club, *U.S. News* posed the question: Is Obama's Immigration Executive Order Legal?" *U.S. News* explained: "In a speech last night, President Barack Obama announced a series of executive orders that will protect up to 5 million undocumented persons from deportation. 'There are actions I have the legal authority to take as president—the same kind of actions taken by Democratic and Republican presidents before me—that will help make our immigration system more fair and more just,' Obama said. Under the president's plan, certain undocumented persons—including those who have children who are U.S. citizens or legal residents—will have the opportunity to receive work documents. He did not extend protection from deportation to the parents of children who are benefiting from his earlier program aimed at so-called 'Dreamers' (young people who were brought to the country illegally as children)." ("Is Obama's Immigration Executive Order Legal?," USNews.com, Debate Club, no date.)

[28]**Two escaped convicts:** Escaping Clinton Correctional Facility in Dannemora, New York, with the help of prison staff, Richard Matt and David Sweat headed north on foot, headed to Canada. Mr. Matt was shot and killed, and Mr. Sweat was also shot but survived, and is now in custody. Both were convicted killers who were considered armed and dangerous, striking fear in the local populace as an army of police officers searched for them.

[29]**Common Core State Standards Initiative:** "Building on the best of existing state standards, the Common Core State Standards provide clear and consistent learning goals to help prepare students for college, career, and life. The standards clearly demonstrate what students are expected to learn at each grade level, so that every parent and teacher can understand and support their learning.

"The standards are:
1. Research and evidence based
2. Clear, understandable, and consistent
3. Aligned with college and career expectations

4. Based on rigorous content and the application of knowledge through higher-order thinking skills

5. Built upon the strengths and lessons of current state standards

6. Informed by other top-performing countries to prepare all students for success in our global economy and society. ("Read the Standards," CoreStandards.org.)

[30]**Trump's renovation of the Old Post Office in D.C.:** The *New York Times* explained that 80 firms showed interest in the renovation, with 10 making a formal proposal. In the end, "Last August, the agency signed a 60-year lease with the Trump Organization to renovate and convert the iconic building into a luxury hotel. Trump formally takes possession on Saturday, allowing work to begin on a $200 million makeover. The deal also includes two 20-year lease renewal options." ("A Trump Makeover for Washington's Old Post Office," by Eugene L. Meyer, NYTimes.com, May 27, 2014.)

[31]**Aging LaGuardia Airport:** The *New York Times* reported that LaGuardia Airport "will be completely rebuilt by 2021," a project that "replaces the airport in its entirety," said Gov. Andrew M. Cuomo of New York. Developer Joseph Sitt, of the Global Gateway Alliance, said it's "a win for the more than 117 million annual passengers that use our airports and for a regional economy that relies on the airports for more than $50 billion in activity." ("LaGuardia Airport to be Overhauled by 2021, Cuomo and Biden Say," by Patrick McGeehan, July 27, 2015.)

# Trump on Politics

## ABORTION

"There are certain things that I don't think can ever be negotiated. Let me put it this way: I am pro-life, and pro-life people will find out that I will be very loyal to them, just as I am loyal to other people. I would be appointing judges that feel the way I feel."

### Source
"CITY ROOM; Trump on Abortion, Swearwords and Handshakes," by Michael Barbaro, *New York Times*, May 3, 2011.

*http://query.nytimes.com/gst/fullpage.html?res=9A03EED71F30F93 0A35756C0A9679D8B63*

### In Context
As his critics point out, Trump's position on abortion has changed from pro-choice to pro-life when it ceased to be an abstract concept and became personalized. As he explained to David Brody of *The Brody File* (CBN News: Blogs, April 8, 2011), "One thing about me, I'm a very honorable guy. I'm pro-life, but I changed my view a number of years ago. One of the reasons I

changed . . . a friend of mine's wife was pregnant, in this case married. She was pregnant and he didn't really want the baby. And he was telling me the story. He was crying as he was telling me the story. He ends up having the baby and the baby is the apple of his eye. It's the greatest thing that's ever happened to him. And you know here's a baby that wasn't going to be let into life. And I heard this, and some other stories, and I'm pro-life . . . [The stories] changed me. Yeah, they changed my view as to that, absolutely."

## AMERICA, A DUMPING GROUND

"When Mexico sends its people, they're not sending their best . . . They're sending people that have lots of problems, and they're bringing those problems with us. They're bringing drugs. They're bringing crime. They're rapists. And some, I assume, are good people."

### Source
"Donald Trump Transcript: 'Our Country Needs a Truly Great Leader,'" by Washington Wire, *Wall Street Journal*, June 16, 2015.

*http://blogs.wsj.com/washwire/2015/06/16/donald-trump-transcript-our-country-needs-a-truly-great-leader/*

### In Context
In a subsequent interview with NBC's Katy Tur, he clarified his comments: "I have many legal immigrants working with me. And many of them come from Mexico. They love me, I love them. I'll create jobs and the Latinos will have jobs they didn't have. I'll do better on that vote than anybody; I will win that vote."

The Latino vote is critical to Trump and the GOP's plans to win the election. As the *Los Angeles Times* pointed out ("Donald Trump's comments offend many U.S. Latinos, but not all," by Kate Linthicum, *Los Angeles Times*, July 23, 2015), "Republicans will probably need a large percentage of the Latino vote if they hope to win the White House. In 2012, Republican nominee Mitt Romney won nearly six in ten white voters but lost the election because African-Americans, Latinos, Asians and other racial minorities overwhelmingly voted for President Obama. Romney drew roughly 27% of the Latino vote, according to exit polls. With the country steadily growing less white, most Republican strategists believe their party needs to significantly improve on Romney's showing among Latinos to have a shot at the presidency."

## APPEAL AND CREDIBILITY

"They see somebody who's going to turn this country around—somebody who has the ability to turn this country around. They're tired of the incompetence. When you see my [financial] statement, you'll be very impressed. That's why it's important. Let's say I was worth $10. People would say, 'Who the [expletive] are you?' You understand? They know my statement. Fortune. My book, *The Art of the Deal*, based on my fortune. If I didn't make a fortune, who the [expletive] is going to buy *The Art of the Deal*? That's why they watched *The Apprentice*, because of my great success."

### Source

"Listening to Donald Trump swear and talk politics on his private plane," by Robert Costa, *Washington Post*, July 12, 2015.

*www.washingtonpost.com/news/post-politics/wp/2015/07/12/ listening-to-donald-trump-swear-and-talk-politics-on-his-private-plane/*

## In Context

A constant theme in Trump's life is that, as he told *Playboy* (March 1990), "I don't want to be president. I'm 100 percent sure. I'd change my mind only if I saw the country continue to go down the tubes." That was twenty-five years ago. In Trump's assessment, the country has indeed continued its downward descent, forcing his hand.

Trump's undeniable success as a businessman is principally what sets him apart from the other presidential aspirants, regardless of party affiliation. As Jeremy Diamond of CNN noted ("Donald Trump jumps in," June 17, 2015), "he flaunted his wealth and success in business as a centerpiece of his presidential platform . . . He pointed out that his wealth and successful business career not only qualified him to be president . . . but that it would allow him to rid himself of the special interests that he said control American politics."

# "BIRTHER" ISSUE

"There is a very large segment of our society who believe that Barack Obama, indeed, was not born in the United States. His grandmother from Kenya stated, on tape, that he was born in Kenya and she was there to watch the birth. His family in Honolulu is fighting over which hospital in Hawaii he was born in—they just don't know.

"He has not been able to produce a 'birth certificate' but merely a totally unsigned 'certificate of live birth'—which is totally different and of very little significance. Unlike a birth certificate, a certificate of live birth is very easy to obtain. Equally of importance, there are no records in Hawaii that a Barack Hussein Obama was born there—no bills, no doctors' names, no nurses' names, no registrations, no payments, etc. As far as the two notices placed in newspapers, many things could have happened, but some feel the grandparents put an ad in order to show that he was a citizen of the U.S. with all of the benefits thereto. Everybody, after all, and especially then, wanted to be a United States citizen. . .

"For some reason, the press protects President Obama beyond anything or anyone I have ever seen. What they don't realize is that if he was not born in the United States, they would have uncovered the greatest 'scam' in the history of our country."

## Source
Letter to the editor, "Donald Trump Responds," *New York Times*, April 8, 2011.

*www.nytimes.com/2011/04/08/opinion/lweb08trump.html?_r=2*

## In Context
Trump, who is well known (among other things) for his criticisms of President Barack Obama, asserts that because there is no birth certificate for the president, he's not a "natural-born" citizen, and thus cannot hold the office of President of the United States. He was born, Trump contends, in Kenya—not Hawaii.

In 2008, the Obama campaign released the president's Certificate of Live Birth, showing he was born in Hawaii. When Trump and others complained this was insufficient documentation, the president authorized the release of his long-form birth certificate on April 27, 2011.

A CNN/Opinion Research Corporation poll "showed that nearly 75% of Americans believe Obama was definitely or probably born in the United States. More than four in 10 Republicans, however, believe he probably or definitely was not born in America." ("CNN Investigation: Obama born in U.S.," by Gary Tuchman, April 25, 2011, *www.cnn.com/2011/POLITICS/04/25/birthers.obama.hawaii/.*)

## BIRTHER ISSUE REVISITED

"I don't talk about that anymore."

### Source

"Watch Donald Trump's Unapologetic Stephen Colbert Interview," by Daniel Kreps, RollingStone.com, September 23, 2015.

*www.rollingstone.com/tv/news/watch-donald-trumps-unapologetic-stephen-colbert-interview-20150923*

### In Context

Trump seems to have realized this issue is taking away attention from his campaign, and so refuses to address it any longer.

## BUSH, GEORGE W.

"I wasn't a huge fan of Bush, as you know . . . I thought he was lost. I thought he was not a great president . . . He certainly wasn't a good president. He got us into Iraq, which by itself was a disaster. He also caused toward the end of his thing a financial problem by allowing exploding mortgages and other things that I predicted. I said you're going to have a huge bubble here. We have another one coming up by the way. I predicted that. You have exploding mortgages. I understood. I made a lot of money because I went in and bought a lot of stuff at the low price after it exploded. But he really gave us Obama. Clinton had a lot of problems with the Monicas of the world and had he not had those problems he would have had a pretty good presidency. Not a great one, but a pretty solid presidency. But that was a disaster and a tremendous distraction."

### Source

"Donald Trump Explains All," by *Time* Staff (Nancy Gibbs, Michael Scherer, and Zeke Miller), Time.com, August 20, 2015.

*http://time.com/4003734/donald-trump-interview-transcript/*

## BUSH, JEB

"And we need a person with a lot of smarts, a lot of cunning and a lot of energy. And Jeb doesn't have that. I think he's a very nice person. If he came president—if he became president, good luck. It's another Bush. It's going to be the same old story."

### Source

"*This Week* Transcript: Donald Trump," interview by George Stephanopoulos, ABC News, August 23, 2015.

*http://abcnews.go.com/Politics/week-transcript-donald-trump/story?id=33203713*

## ICAHN, CARL

"I'd say, 'Carl, congratulations, handle China.' I'd get other guys like Carl. I'd say, 'Good luck, here's Japan.' Believe me, we will do so well. We will make so much."

## Source

"Feeling the pre-debate fervor," by Kathleen Parker, *Washington Post*, August 5, 2015.

Accessible to HighBeam.com subscribers at *www.highbeam.com/doc/1P2-38588017.html*.

## In Context

Trump has long asserted that America is losing the trade wars, principally because we don't take a strong stance. In *Trump: Surviving at the Top*, he recommends an "all-star panel that would oversee America's negotiations with Japan, Europe, and other areas needing attention." Calling on people whom he knows—all tough negotiators—he cites, among them, Carl Icahn, then the head of Trans World Airlines.

As Trump told *Playboy* (March 1990), "I think if we had people from the business community—the Carl Icahns, the Ross Perots—negotiating some of our foreign policy, we'd have respect around the world."

# BUSH, JEB (AGAIN)

"How can I be tied with Jeb Bush? He's terrible. He's weak on immigration. Sanctuary cities. Did you know that he had five of them in Florida when he was governor? . . . I don't see [Bush] as a factor."

## Source

"Trump on Jeb Bush: 'I don't see him as a factor,'" by Reena Flores, CBSNews.com, July 11, 2015.

*www.cbsnews.com/news/election-2016-donald-trump-jeb-bush-i-dont-see-him-as-a-factor/*

### In Context

A savvy career politician, Jeb Bush chooses his words carefully, saying that Trump's "harsh tone is wrong" and pointing the finger to him obliquely, saying that "I don't think politicians should prey on that fear and angst . . . To win, and to go the right way, we have to unite rather than divide." ("Jeb Bush Cautions Donald Trump on Preying on Voters' 'Fear and Angst,'" by Michael Barbaro, *New York Times*, August 4, 2015.)

## CHERISHING WOMEN

"Women's health issues to me are very important. I cherish women. I mean, my mother was this incredible woman. I have great children. I have a great wife. I cherish women. I understand the importance of women. I have such respect for women. I have many executives in my organization that are women that frankly get paid more than many of my men executives. I mean, they've done great with me. Early on when I was building major towers, I had women in charge of a couple of them. And really big ones and really important ones. And that was unheard of in the construction industry. If you look back 30 years, that was, like, totally unheard of. So I understand women. And women's health issues are very important to me. If you look at Jeb Bush from last week when he was essentially saying, 'Let's not give money to women's health issues,' he's made so many flubs I don't even understand it."

### Source

"Donald Trump on *Meet the Press*, annotated," by Chris Cillizza, WashingtonPost.com, August 17, 2015.

*www.washingtonpost.com/news/the-fix/wp/2015/08/17/donald-trump-on-meet-the-press-annotated/*

# CHINA AND NORTH KOREA

"I would make China respect us because China has extreme control over North Korea . . . And I would say, 'China, you better go in there, and you better do something' because economically it could cause China—Just like I have the Chinese banks in my buildings, they listen to me, they respect me. Chinas has almost complete control over North Korea. China will do that. And if they don't do that, they have to suffer economically because we have the engine that makes China work. You know, without the United States or without China sucking out all our money and our jobs China would collapse in about two minutes."

## Source

"Trump gets down to business on *60 Minutes*," interview by Scott Pelley, airdate September 27, 2015.

*www.cbsnews.com/news/donald-trump-60-minutes-scott-pelley/*

# CHINESE TRADE IMBALANCE

"Look, China is like Mexico. They're taking advantage of the United States. They're laughing all the way to the bank. Of course they're going to respond, and they said essentially, 'Oh no, we love our trading partner, the United States.' Well, of course they should love us, they're making a fortune off of us. But we make nothing off of them. We get nothing out of that deal, believe me. That would change if I become president."

## Source

"Donald Trump: I'm No 'Apprentice' When It Comes to Israel," by Jacob Karmas/JNS.org; Algemeiner.com, June 29, 2015.

*www.algemeiner.com/2015/06/29/donald-trump-im-no-apprentice-when-it-comes-to-israel-interview/*

### In Context

As Trump sees it, our country's fortunes, and misfortunes, are inextricably tied into our economic dealings with China, whom he sees as manipulative, especially when it comes to currency.

As Trump was quoted by Mark Hensch in TheHill.com (August 12, 2015), "They're just destroying us. They keep devaluating their currency until they get it right. They're doing a big cut in the yuan, and that's going to be devastating for us. China has gotten rich off us. China has rebuilt itself with the money it's sucked out of the United States and the jobs that it's sucked out of the United States."

Watching the international turmoil of stock markets worldwide as the world reacted to Chinese currency manipulation of the yuan, causing a 1,000 point drop on the Dow, Trump tweeted, "As I have long stated, we are so tied with China and Asia that their markets are now taking the U.S. market down. Get smart U.S.A. . . . Markets are crashing—all caused by poor planning and allowing China and Asia to dictate the agenda. This could get very messy! Vote Trump" (August 24, 2015).

# CHRISTIAN

"So you tell me about religious liberty and freedom. The Christians are being treated horribly because we have nobody to represent the Christians. Believe me, if I run and I win, I will be the greatest representative of the Christians they've had in a long time."

## Source

"Donald Trump Tells *Brody File*: As President 'I will be the greatest representative of the Christians they've had in a long time,'" by David Brody, CBN News: Blogs, May 20, 2015.

*http://blogs.cbn.com/thebrodyfile/archive/2015/05/20/donald-trump-tells-brody-file-as-president--i-will.aspx*

## In Context

At a July 11, 2015, speech in Las Vegas, Trump, a Protestant, talked about the persecution of Christians—he's complained that the Obama administration favors Muslim immigrants over Christian immigrants. "If you're from Syria and you're a Christian, you cannot come into this country. And they're the ones that are being persecuted. If you're Islamic and you come in, hard to believe, you can come in so easily. In fact, it's one of our main groups of people that are coming in. Not that we should discriminate against one or the other. But if you're Christian, you cannot get into the country. You cannot get in. I thought that was unbelievable. We have to do something about it."

PolitiFact.com (Louis Jacobson, July 20, 2015) disagrees: "Between Oct. 1, 2014, and July 17, 2015, according to federal data, 859 Sunni Muslims, five Shiite Muslims and 42 people identified only as 'Muslim' arrived in the United States as refugees from Syria, for a total of 906. Meanwhile, 28 Christians arrived from Syria. (Other arrivals included two atheists, two of the Baha'i Faith and one with no stated religion.) . . . Our ruling: Trump said that 'if you're from Syria and you're a Christian, you cannot come into this country' as a refugee. This is wrong on its face—a small number of Syrian Christians have been admitted as refugees over the past nine months—and also false in spirit, since there is nothing in the United States' laws or regulations that discriminates against Christian refugees. We rate the claim false."

# CLINTON, HILLARY

"You talk about Teflon and they have been skirting the law for years in so many different elements but it is amazing that she's getting away with it and they talk like she's going to be running, she's going to be the candidate. I was watching some of the pundits the other day, even the Republicans, even the conservative guys they are talking like it's going to be Hillary and they don't speak of it like I speak of it. I'm very surprised that they are not tougher with what she did with e-mails because it is really a criminal act. You know, she got a subpoena from the United States Congress and after she got the subpoena she deleted a lot of the e-mails. I mean that was a combination. So, what she has done is incredible and it is incredible to me that they are talking about her as the candidate so routinely and you see that. You know they talk about Hillary as a candidate, but what she did I think was illegal."

## Source

"Donald Trump on Things 2016," by Hugh Hewitt, transcript, HughHewitt.com, August 3, 2015.

*www.hughhewitt.com/donald-trump-on-things-2016/*

## In Context

CNN Politics ("Trump on Clinton," by Eric Bradner, July 26, 2015) quotes from Jake Tapper's phone interview with Trump. He feels that Clinton's usage of a private computer server for personal e-mails is far more heinous than General Petraeus's actions. "The fact is that what she has done is criminal. What she did is far worse than what General Petraeus did and he's gone down in disgrace. What he did is not as bad as what Hillary Clinton did, and it's similar. But it's not as bad. I mean, she got rid of her server, he never did anything like that." CNN notes that Petraeus "pleaded guilty to a misdemeanor charge of mishandling classified information." (He gave bound volumes of classified information to his biographer-cum-mistress, Paula Broadwell.)

# COLLINS, GAIL

*On April 2, 2011, Gail Collins, a* New York Times *journalist, published a column titled "Donald Trump Gets Weirder." In the piece, she sarcastically lambasts him: "Trump's main argument for why he should be taken seriously as a presidential contender is his business success. Has Obama ever hosted a long-running reality series? Owned a bankruptcy-bound chain of casinos? Put his name on a flock of really unattractive high-rise apartments? No! . . . During one down period, I referred to him in print as a 'financially embattled thousandaire' and he sent me a copy of the column with my picture circled and 'The Face of a Dog!' written over it."*

*Collins's comments pinked the angry bull: Trump fired back with a letter to the editor. He wrote:* "Even before Gail Collins was with the *New York Times*, she has written nasty and derogatory articles about me. Actually, I have great respect for Ms. Collins in that she has survived so long with so little talent. Her storytelling ability and word usage (coming from me, who has written many best sellers) is not at a very high level. More importantly, her facts are wrong!"

## Source

Letter to the editor, "Donald Trump Responds," *New York Times*, April 8, 2011.

*www.nytimes.com/2011/04/08/opinion/lweb08trump.html?_r=0*

### In Context

In *Trump: Never Give Up*, Chapter 38 is titled, "When You're Attacked, Bite Back." Trump bit back hard when Collins attacked him. In his book, Trump writes at length about a *New York Times* writer named Timothy L. O'Brien who published *TrumpNation: The Art of Being The Donald* (2005). Trump, who had given O'Brien unparalleled access to him to ensure "his facts would be correct," was gobsmacked when the book was published, because "I realized there's a difference between bad news and evil. This guy was despicable. His intent was defamation." But this was not a battle that Trump won. The *Hollywood Reporter* (Eriq Gardner, September 8, 2011) reported that, "A New Jersey appeals court has affirmed a lower court's ruling to dismiss a defamation lawsuit brought by Donald Trump . . ." In response, Trump told the *Reporter* that the nation's libel laws "have never been fair."

## CONSERVATIVE—OR NOT

"Well, you know, you could say that about Ronald Reagan, because Ronald Reagan was a Democrat with a very, very liberal lean. And he actually became a Republican who was fairly conservative. I wouldn't say he was the most conservative, but fairly.

"And he talked about how he evolved as he got older. And I have also. And don't forget, I—when you label me—I was never a politician. So, it never really mattered what people called me. It didn't make any difference. Also, I was in Manhattan, where everybody is Democrat. If you get the Democratic nomination for city council or anything, that means you won the election, even though the election hasn't taken place. It was like automatic.

"So, I was from an area that was all Democrat. And, frankly, over the years, I have—and especially as I have gotten more and more involved—I have evolved. And I have taken positions that are different than the past. And I feel strongly about them."

### Source

"*Face the Nation* transcript August 23, 2015: Trump, Christie & Cruz," interview by CBS host John Dickerson, CBSNews.com.

*www.cbsnews.com/news/face-the-nation-transcripts-august-23-2015-trump-christie-cruz/*

## DEATH PENALTY RESTORATION

*Trump paid $85,000 for ads in four New York City newspapers after an attack on a woman jogger and others in Central Park on April 19, 1989, perpetrated by "muggers and murderers . . . They should be forced to suffer and, when they kill, they should be executed for their crimes."*

"I hate seeing this country go to hell. We're laughed at by the rest of the world. In order to bring law and order back into our cities, we need the death penalty and authority given back to the police. I got fifteen thousand positive letters on the death-penalty ad. I got ten negative or slightly negative ones . . . When a man or woman cold-bloodedly murders, he or she should pay. It sets an example. Nobody can make the argument that the death penalty isn't a deterrent. Either it will be brought back swiftly or our society will rot away. It is rotting away."

### Source

"Donald Trump," by Glenn Plaskin, *Playboy*, March 1990.

## In Context

Trump is unflinching on the subject of harsh punishment for convicted criminals. He's for capital punishment, long sentences, tough anti-crime policies, and holding judges accountable for their decisions—he calls them "forgiving judges" (*The America We Deserve*). In that book, Trump writes: "Civilized people don't put up with barbaric behavior . . . Would it have been civilized to put Hitler in prison? No—it would have been an affront to civilization . . . I don't care if the victim is a CEO or a floor sweeper. A life is a life, and if you criminally take an innocent life you'd better be prepared to forfeit your own."

In the same book, he explains his position on the death penalty: "To point out the extremely obvious, 100 percent of the people who are executed never commit another crime. And it seems self-evident (we can't put numbers to this) that a lot of people who might otherwise commit a capital crime are convinced not to do so because they know there's a chance they could die for it."

The five young men who were accused of the attack on the Central Park jogger were subsequently convicted and spent between six and thirteen years in prison. In 2002 another man, a convicted murderer already in prison, confessed to the rape and said he had acted alone. The state, based on confirming DNA evidence (his semen on the jogger's sock), vacated the sentences of the men originally convicted of the crime. In 2014 the city of New York settled a lawsuit the men brought against it for $41 million.

From the *New York Times* ("Trump Draws Criticism for Ad He Ran After Jogger Attack," by Michael Wilson, October 23, 2002): "On May 1, 1989, Donald J. Trump took out full-page advertisements in four local newspapers calling for the return of the death penalty. Mr. Trump said he wanted the 'criminals of every age' who were accused of beating and raping a jogger in Central Park 12 days earlier 'to be afraid.'"

Critics of the death penalty point to such cases as proof that human frailty can, and does, condemn innocent men to unwarranted deaths; the critics advocate life in prison, an alternative that provides a life-saving option, instead of an irreversible death sentence.

# THE DEBATES

"As for preparing for the debates, I am who I am. I don't know. I've never debated before. I'm not a debater. I get things done. I have no idea how I'll do. Maybe I'll do terribly. Maybe I'll do great . . . Well, I'm not a debater. These politicians—I always say they're all talk, no action. They debate all the time. They go out and they debate every night. I don't debate. I build—I've created tremendous jobs. I've built a great company. I do a lot of things."

## Source

"*This Week* Transcript: Donald Trump," interview by Tom Llamas, ABC News, August 2, 2015.

*http://abcnews.go.com/Politics/week-transcript-donald-trump/ story?id=32829376*

## In Context

The politicians' strategy before the televised public debate was to have their staffs work up position papers on every possible subject, so they could rattle off facts and figures to buttress their position. The *Washington Post* (Aug. 6, 2015) noted that "Jeb Bush has been practicing all summer . . . Ted Cruz spent this week ensconced with advisors."

Trump, though his staff prepared position papers, has preferred a wait-and-see posture. "I'll have to feel it out, see where everyone else is coming from. I'd prefer no conflict, no infighting, but if they hit me, I'll hit them harder. It's all going to depend on the moment. You watch. I am going to keep it on a high level. I have a lot of respect for them." ("Trump Gets Center Stage, and Foes Get Chance to Topple Him," by Robert Costa and Philip Rucker, *Washington Post*, August 6, 2015.)

## DEFEATING ISIS

"I have an absolute way of defeating ISIS, and it would be decisive and quick and it would be very beautiful. Very surgical . . ." (*Military on the ground? Drone strikes?*) "If I tell you right now, everyone else is going to say: 'Wow, what a great idea.' You're going to have ten candidates going to use it and they're going to forget where it came from. Which is me."

### Source

"Donald Trump's insane interview with the *Des Moines Register*, annotated," by Jon Green, AMERICAblog, June 2, 2015.

*http://americablog.com/2015/06/donald-trump-insane-interview-with-the-des-moines-register-annotated.html*

### In Context

If there's any easy solution—a decisive strike—that will take out ISIS, the U.S. military and its coalition of partners would welcome it. But, as with all things in war, there are seldom simple, surgical solutions: After getting rid of Saddam Hussein, who held an iron grip on Iraq, and whose reign precluded intrusion of terrorist groups seeking to take root in his country, a power vacuum was created. As Majid Karimi, a Middle East journalist pointed out, "ISIS . . . has its roots in the al-Qaeda group in Iraq after the

Saddam regime fell. Al-Baghdadi, a Sunni cleric extremist, was leader of al-Qaeda in Iraq until 2010 and then he abandoned them and created ISIS, when Islamist groups started to fight Bashar [al-]Assad . . . Indeed, ISIS can take advantage of the different policies of various regional and international players in the short term. It is a complex matter with many factions and players behind the scenes." ("What makes it difficult to fight ISIS?" by Majid Karimi, Rappler.com, April 14, 2015.)

As Karimi points out, there are no simple answers, no quick solutions, no easy fixes—despite what Trump, or anyone else, asserts.

## DEFLECTION

*When NBC News' Katy Tur questioned Trump on his views about birtherism, she concluded: "You led the birther movement. You sent investigators out to Hawaii to find out whether or not Obama, who you said, was not born here. He released his birth certificate."*

"If you believe that, that's fine. I don't care. I'm about jobs. I'm about security. I'm about fixing the military. I'm about taking care of our vets. I am about things. You don't have to bring up old subjects. Whether [Obama] did or not, who knows? A lot of people disagree with you on that."

### Source

"Watch the Full, Unedited Donald Trump Interview," NBC News, video, July 8, 2015.

*www.nbcnews.com/video/watch-the-full-unedited-donald-trump-interview-480244291643*

## In Context

During the first Republican presidential debate (August 6, 2015), Megyn Kelly attacked Trump on the grounds that his offhand comments about women show he doesn't have the "temperament of a man we should elect as president." Rather than engaging her on the question—a no-win situation where he'd likely get tangled up in the barbwire—Trump switched gears and, after pointing out that he saved his insults "only [for] Rosie O'Donnell," which got a big laugh, he deflected her question by attacking it. As CNN noted, "Trump didn't flinch and didn't apologize." He instead cited the problem as political correctness. "I don't frankly have time for total political correctness. And to be honest with you, this country doesn't have time either."

# FIORINA, CARLY

"*Look* at that face! Would anyone *vote* for that? Can you imagine that, the face of our next *president*?! I mean, she's a woman, and I'm not s'posed ta say bad things, but really, folks, come on. Are we *serious*?"

## Source

"Trump Seriously," by Paul Solotaroff, *Rolling Stone*, September 9, 2015. *www.rollingstone.com/politics/news/trump-seriously-20150909*

## In Context

At the second Republican debate, on September 16, 2015, Fiorina drew the largest applause of the night when she refused to address Trump's comments in *Rolling Stone*, saying simply: "I think women all over this country heard very clearly what Mr. Trump said."

Trump's response, to which she did not respond at all: "I think she's got a beautiful face and I think she's a beautiful woman."

Trump can be his own worst enemy, shooting himself in his foot. His comment in *Rolling Stone* served no useful purpose, except to alienate a large population of female voters who feel they are still being judged on their looks alone—a perception that Trump's comments fueled.

## FOURTEENTH AMENDMENT

"Well, first of all, the—the Fourteenth Amendment says very, very clearly to a lot of great legal scholars—not television scholars, but legal scholars—that it is wrong. It can be corrected with an act of Congress, probably doesn't even need that.

"A woman gets pregnant. She's nine months, she walks across the border, she has the baby in the United States, and we take care of the baby for 85 years. I don't think so.

"And by the way, Mexico and almost every other country anywhere in the world doesn't have that. We're the only ones dumb enough, stupid enough to have it. And people—and by the way, this is not just with respect to Mexico. They are coming from Asia to have babies here, and all of a sudden, we have to take care of the babies for the life of the baby.

"The Fourteenth Amendment, it reads properly, you can go and—it's probably going to be have to be checked—go through a process of court, probably ends up at the Supreme Court, but there are a lot of great legal scholars that say that is not correct.

"And in my opinion, it makes absolutely no—we're the only—one of the only countries, we're going to take care of those babies for 70, 75, 80, 90 years? I don't think so."

## Source

"Transcript: Read the Full Text of the Second Republican Debate," by Ryan Teague Beckwith, Time.com, September 16, 2015.

*http://time.com/4037239/second-republican-debate-transcript-cnn/*

## In Context

Trump is referring to the phenomenon of women deliberately traveling to the U.S. on a short-term basis to have babies in the U.S., thus automatically granting them citizenship for life. As *Time* (Hannah Beech, "I Want an American Baby!," November 27, 2013) pointed out, "The U.S. is one of the few nations where simply being born on its soil confers citizenship on a newborn. That policy has spawned a birth-tourism industry, in which pregnant foreigners flock to American hospitals to secure U.S. passports for their babies. Although the foreign couple can't acquire U.S. nationality themselves, once their American-born offspring turn 21 they can theoretically sponsor their parents for future U.S. citizenship . . . More rich Chinese than ever are sending their families and money abroad . . . All of which has led to a proliferation of so-called anchor babies. At least 10,000 such Chinese babies were born in America last year, according to an estimate by an online platform dedicated to monitoring and rating confinement centers for Chinese women giving birth in the States."

# GOOD IMMIGRANTS

"We also want people of talent to come into the country. We want people to go to our colleges. You to go Harvard, you go to Wharton, you go to Stanford, and you are immediately thrown out as soon as you're finished getting a degree. You can be number one in your class at Princeton and be thrown out of the country, and you have—you're forced to go to work in China, where you want—and you want to be in this—you want to be in our country.

"I will have that changed and changed quickly. We want people of talent."

### Source

"*Face the Nation* transcript August 23, 2015: Trump, Christie & Cruz," interview by CBS host John Dickerson, CBSNews.com, August 23, 2015.

*www.cbsnews.com/news/face-the-nation-transcripts-august-23-2015-trump-christie-cruz/*

## GOVERNMENT BEING RUN AS A BUSINESS

"The government needs to be run as a business. Negotiating is an important skill in business and diplomatic relations and we need dealmakers with this ability. Also, leadership is crucial and I believe we don't have the best leaders. Teams are important but there has to be strong leadership. As an entrepreneur, I understand this concept and it applies to government as well."

### Source

"Donald Trump's Advice for Millennials," by Geoffrey James, Inc.com, January 22, 2014.

*www.inc.com/geoffrey-james/donald-trumps-advice-for-millennials.html*

### In Context

Trump feels Washington needs immediate and drastic reform, and people like him—tested in the rough-and-tumble world of high finance and business—are the negotiators we need to cut deals that favor the U.S. "We need people in Washington that know how to make a deal," Trump said to activists in New Hampshire. ("Trump says his business experience would play well in government," by Kathleen Ronayne, Associated Press, MSNBC .com, March 19, 2015.) He added that, unlike the other candidates running for office, who want to cut Social Security and Medicaid, he wouldn't because "I would make this country so rich that you wouldn't have to cut it."

## GREAT WALL OF TRUMP

"I would build a wall when necessary. I would build a wall, and Mexico would pay for it. Mexico's made a tremendous amount of money off the stupidity of the United States. They're continuing to make even more money. Every day they make more and more money. Mexico will pay for that wall. The only good news is I know how to build it for the proper price, but it'll be a real wall. It's not going to be a wall that [is] like a sieve where people can walk right through it. This will be a real wall.

"And yes, you're right, Mexico will pay for it. Mexico's making a fortune off the United States. Again, I love Mexico. I love the Mexican people. But they're taking advantage of the stupidity and the very stupid negotiators and politicians that we have in the United States. You're very lucky to have the people that you have negotiating."

### Source

"Transcript: Donald Trump Exclusive Telemundo Interview," by José Díaz-Balart, NBCUniversal MediaVillage, Noticiero Telemundo, June 25, 2015.

*https://www.nbcumv.com/news/transcript%C2%A0-donald-trump-exclusive-telemundo-interview*

### In Context

Reuters ("Trump says would raise visa fees to pay for Mexican border wall," by Toni Clarke and Christine Murray, August 16, 2015) summarized Trump's immigration plan, including forcing Mexico to pay for a border wall: (1) If Mexico doesn't agree to pay for the wall, institute fees for temporary visas; (2) deport undocumented immigrants; (3) rescind Obama's executive orders on immigration; (4) impound remittance payments from illegal immigrants; (5) increase port of entry fees, cut foreign aid, and impose tariffs. Trump concludes: "The Mexican government has taken the United States to the cleaners. They are responsible for this problem, and they must help pay to clean it up."

## GUN CONTROL

"I am a life member of the NRA and am proud of their service in protecting our right to keep and bear arms. The NRA's efforts to stop dangerous, gun-banning legislation and regulation is invaluable. The media focus on those efforts overshadows the great work the NRA does on behalf of safety and conservation.

"I have a permit to carry and, living in New York, I know firsthand the challenges law-abiding citizens have in exercising their Second Amendment rights. My most trusted sources are my sons, Don Jr. and Eric. They are fantastic sportsmen and are deeply involved in hunting, competitive shooting, and habitat conservation.

"The Trump family will stay vigilant in our support of the right to keep and bear arms. And given today's threats across the United States it is as important now as ever. National security begins in our homes. All citizens must have the ability to protect themselves, their families, and their property. The Second

Amendment is a right, not a privilege. Our safety and defense [are] embodied in the Second Amendment and I will always protect this most important right."

## Source

"Donald Trump Talks: Gun Control, Assault Weapons, Gun Free Zones & Self Defense," by Fredy Riehl, Ammoland.com; Alex Jones's Infowars.com, July 11, 2015.

*www.infowars.com/donald-trump-talks-gun-control-assault-weapons-gun-free-zones-self-defense/*

# HEALTHCARE

"I'm also a moralist. You heard what I said today about healthcare. I said, I'm sorry, folks, but we have to take care of people that don't have money. I know it's not the conservative thing to say, but I got a standing ovation—and these were very conservative people. We can't let people down when they can't get any medical care, when they're sick and don't have money to go to a doctor. You help them."

## Source

"Donald Trump interview: Real-estate mogul talks press and politics aboard his private plane," by Robert Costa, *Independent*, July 13, 2015.

*www.independent.co.uk/news/people/donald-trump-interview-real-estate-mogul-talks-press-and-politics-aboard-his-private-plane-10386260.html*

## In Context

In *Time to Get Tough* (2011), Trump explains that although he's against the Affordable Care Act (Obamacare), he's an advocate for universal healthcare. "I'm a conservative on most issues but a liberal on health. It is an unacceptable but accurate fact that the number of uninsured Americans has risen to forty-two million . . . Our people are our greatest asset. We must take care of our own. We must have universal healthcare . . .

"There is already a system in place—the Federal Employees Health Benefits Program—that can act as a guide for all healthcare reform. It operates through a centralized agency that offers considerable range of choice. While this is a government program, it is also very much market-based. It allows 620 private insurance companies to compete for this market. Once a year participants can choose from plans which vary in benefits and costs."

## ILLEGAL IMMIGRANTS: A ROUNDUP

*When asked by Pelley, "Are you serious about deporting 12 million illegal immigrants?"* "Well, nobody knows the number. But the answer is—you just said it: they're illegal immigrants. They're here illegally . . . If they've done well, they're going out and they're coming back in legally . . . We're rounding 'em up in a very humane way, in a very nice way. And they're going to be happy because they want to be legalized. And, by the way, I know it doesn't sound nice, but not everything is nice . . . When I talk about the wall, and I've said it before, we're going to have a tremendous, beautiful, wide-open door, nice big door. We *want* people to come into the country."

### Source

"Trump gets down to business on *60 Minutes*," interview by Scott Pelley, airdate September 27, 2015.

*www.cbsnews.com/news/donald-trump-60-minutes-scott-pelley/*

# INDEPENDENCE

"I have been a very big contributor to many, many people of all size for many, many years. I don't want lobbyists. I don't want special interests, but certainly people—we have lot of money coming in.

"A woman sends in $7.23 the other day. It was cute. She writes this beautiful little letter. That's what she had. But we have lot of small contributors. I would even take big contributors, as long as they don't expect anything, because the only people that can expect something from me is going to be the people that want to see our country be great again.

"Those are the only people. So, certainly, I would take—I actually like the idea of investing in a campaign, but it has to be no strings attached. I don't want any strings attached. You know, these lobbyists come in. I turned down $5 million last week from a very important lobbyist, because there are total strings attached to a thing like that.

"He's going to come to me in a year or two years and he's going to want something for a country that he represents or for a company that he represents. That's the kind of money I won't take."

## Source

"*Face the Nation* transcript August 23, 2015: Trump, Christie & Cruz," interview by CBS host John Dickerson, CBSNews.com, August 23, 2015.

*www.cbsnews.com/news/face-the-nation-transcripts-august-23-2015-trump-christie-cruz/*

# IMMIGRATION POLICY

"We have some really bad dudes right here in this country and we're getting them out. We're sending them back where they came from . . . The bad ones are going to get out. Then, from that point on, we're going to look very, very strongly at what we do. And I'm going to formulate a plan that I think people are going to be happy with . . . We're going to see what we're going to see . . . We're going to take the high ground; we're going to do what's right. Some are going to have a go, and some—hey, we're just going to see what happens. It's a very, very big subject, and a very complicated subject."

## Source

"Donald Trump's Troubles Are Just Beginning," by John Cassidy, *New Yorker*, July 28, 2015.

*www.newyorker.com/news/john-cassidy/donald-trumps-troubles-are-just-beginning*

## In Context

According to the Pew Research Center, as of 2014, there were 11.3 million unauthorized immigrants in the United States, with Mexicans making up 52 percent. Illegal immigrants make up 5.1 percent of our total work force (8.1 million working or looking for work), and in 2012, about 7 percent of the K–12 students have at least one unauthorized immigrant parent.

Compounding the problem: the porous border between Mexico and the U.S., which guarantees that even when deported, Mexicans simply cross back over the border, seeking refuge in sanctuary cities where the law protects them from disclosure of their immigrant status when arrested.

In *Time to Get Tough: Making America #1 Again*, Trump laid out a detailed plan with physical, legal, and political constraints to stem the flow of illegal immigrants: build a border fence, hire 25,000 more border agents, use Predator drones, enforce immigration law, dispense with detention centers that he feels are more like hotels than jails, oppose the DREAM Act (no generous discounts for college tuition), and change the law that grants U.S. citizenship to children born here, regardless of their parents' legal status.

More recently, in a position paper posted on Trump's campaign website (*www.donaldjtrump.com*), he's updated his views, which center on three key points: "(1) A nation without borders is not a nation. There must be a wall across the southern border. (2) A nation without laws is not a nation. Laws passed in accordance with our Constitutional system of government must be enforced. (3) A nation that does not serve its citizens is not a nation. Any immigration plan must improve jobs, wages and security for all Americans." (Positions: "Immigration Reform That Will Make America Great Again.")

The basic plan includes: "Make Mexico pay for the wall . . . Defend the laws and Constitution of the United States . . . Triple the number of ICE officers . . . Nationwide e-verify . . . Mandatory return of all criminal aliens . . . Detention—not catch-and-release . . . Defund sanctuary cities . . . Enhanced penalties for overstaying a visa . . . Cooperate with local gang task forces . . . End birthright citizenship."

Trump's incendiary remarks about illegal immigrants, principally from Mexico, predictably led to a public outcry, especially among the Hispanic community.

Trump feels that in the upcoming general election, Hispanics will vote for him in droves, based on a poll drawn from a few dozen Hispanic Republicans. An NBC News/*Wall Street Journal* poll, drawn on 250 Hispanics, paints a different picture: 13 percent are positive on Trump, 14 percent are negative, and 61 percent are very negative, totaling 75 percent. ("Shock Poll: Latinos really dislike Donald Trump," by Philip Bump, *Washington Post*, August 3, 2015.)

Ruth Marcus, writing in the *Washington Post* ("The false assumptions underlying Trump's immigration plan," August 18, 2015), cites the Hamilton Project report, which concluded: "The consensus of the economics literature is that the taxes paid by immigrants and their descendants exceed the benefits they receive—that on balance they are a net positive for the federal budget." She added, "Illegal immigrants aren't entitled to welfare, food stamps, Medicare or Social Security or unemployment benefits. Indeed, they often pay federal taxes and contribute more than $12 billion annually to Social Security alone without being able to collect."

# ISRAEL

"The only [candidate] that's going to give real support to Israel is me. The rest of them are all talk, no action. They're politicians. I've been loyal to Israel from the day I was born. My father, Fred Trump, was loyal to Israel before me. The only one that's going to give Israel the kind of support it needs is Donald Trump.

"I know so many people from Israel. I have so many friends in Israel. First of all, the Israelis are great businesspeople. They have a natural instinct for business and their start-ups are fantastic. I deal with the Israelis all the time, and I deal with people who are Jewish all the time, whether they are Israeli or not."

## Source

"Donald Trump: I'm No 'Apprentice' When it Comes to Israel," by Jacob Karmas, JNS.org; Algemeiner.com, June 29, 2015.

*www.algemeiner.com/2015/06/29/donald-trump-im-no-apprentice-when-it-comes-to-israel-interview/*

# "JACKASS" ACCUSATION

"Am I supposed to say it's okay to call me a jackass? You have to fight back."

## Source

"Donald Trump Slams Anderson Cooper During Interview: 'The People Don't Trust You'—Watch Now!," by Francesca Bacardi, July 23, 2015.

*www.eonline.com/news/679254/donald-trump-slams-anderson-cooper-during-interview-the-people-don-t-trust-you-watch-now*

## In Context

On *CBS This Morning* (July 21, 2015), Senator Lindsey Graham said: "I don't care if he drops out. Stay in the race, just stop being a jackass. You don't have to run for president and be the world's biggest jackass." Later that day, to CNN's Kate Bolduan, Graham elaborated: "He's becoming a jackass at a time when we need to have a serious debate about the future of the party and the country. This is a line he's crossed, and this is the beginning of the end of Donald Trump . . . I am really pissed."

Trump, in a *Playboy* interview (March 1990) explained that "when somebody tries to sucker-punch me, when they're after my ass, I push back a hell of a lot harder than I was pushed in the first place. If somebody tries to push me around, he's going to pay a price. Those people don't come back for seconds. I don't like being pushed around or taken advantage of."

The price Graham paid was being the target of Trump's attacks. Trump, who had given $2,600 as a campaign contribution to Graham for his 2014 re-election bid, asked "What's this guy? A beggar?" Trump then shared Graham's cell phone number with an audience, and spoke of him: "When you register zero in the polls, what the hell, they have nothing to lose." ("'Jackass,' 'idiot': Graham, Trump trade barbs," by Andrew Shain, TheState.com, July 21, 2015.)

Graham subsequently discarded his flip phone, bought a smartphone, and changed his private cell phone number.

## JOB CREATION

*To then-NBC News White House correspondent Chris Wallace, Trump said*: "I employ thousands and thousands of people that wouldn't have jobs if it weren't for things that I've built. I mean, I employ, probably, 25,000 or 30,000 people, and that—these are things that I've done over the last four- or five-year period, Chris, and I think that a lot of people are very thankful for it." (CNN.com reports that "The Trump Organization employs 22,000 people" in "Fact Check: Is Donald Trump a small business?," by the CNN Wire Staff, CNNPolitics.com, October 5, 2012.)

### Source

"Video Flashback: In '88 Interview, NBC Pushed Donald Trump on Presidential Run; Chided His Wealth," by Rich Noyes, Newsbusters.org, July 17, 2015.

*http://newsbusters.org/blogs/nb/rich-noyes/2015/07/17/video-flashback-88-interview-nbc-pushed-donald-trump-presidential-run*

## KELLY, MEGYN

*On August 6, 2015, at the first Republican presidential debate, Fox moderator Megyn Kelly hit Trump with this statement: "You've called women you don't like 'fat pigs,' 'dogs,' slobs, and disgusting animals." Trump countered, "Only Rosie O'Donnell." She responded, "No, it wasn't. For the record, it*

*was well beyond Rosie O'Donnell. Your Twitter account has several dispar-*
*aging comments about women's looks. You once told a contestant on [The]*
Celebrity Apprentice *it would be a pretty picture to see her on her knees.*
*Does that sound to you like the temperament of a man we should elect as*
*president?"*

"I think the big problem this country has is being politically correct. I've
been challenged by so many people and I don't frankly have time for total
political correctness . . . I've been very nice to you, although I could probably
maybe not be based on the way you have treated me. But I wouldn't do that."

*The next day, on MSNBC's* Morning Joe, *Trump clarified his comments*:
"The question on the women, I didn't say many of those things. I don't
remember that on *The Apprentice*, and I don't remember some of these words,
to be honest with you. In fact, I'm going to have somebody call up and find
out where these words came from."

The simmering tempest in a teapot came to a full boil, but Fox's CEO
turned the heat down by calling Trump to tell him that we "can resolve this
now, or we can go to war." At the end of the day, the dogs of war were kept
at bay.

## KRAUTHAMMER, CHARLES

*The columnist Charles Krauthammer, who is paralyzed from the waist down,*
*attacked Trump as a "rodeo clown." In response, in an NBC News interview,*
*Trump said,* "Then I get called by a guy that can't buy a pair of pants, I get
called names?

"Charles Krauthammer is a totally overrated person who really dis-
likes me personally—I've never met him. He's a totally overrated guy,
doesn't know what he's doing, he was totally in favor of the war in Iraq,

he wanted to go into Iraq and, you know, stay there forever. So these are overrated people, I see who it is, you can mention name after name. By the way, are you going to mention the ones that do like Trump? You don't do that do you?"

## Source

"Donald Trump Insults Disabled Columnist in Interview," by Dieter Holger, Inquisitr.com, July 11, 2015.

*www.inquisitr.com/2244736/donald-trump-insults-disabled-columnist/*

## In Context

Trump's riposte should come as no surprise to anyone who knows his style of verbal fighting. When attacked, he goes on the counterattack. He comes across as an equal opportunity offender because he's not politically correct: He calls them as he sees them—a trait that has endeared him to voters who prefer straight talk to political obfuscation, and one of the reasons he's riding high in the polls—and doesn't feel that he should take flung dung from his critics who make personal remarks about him.

## LEADERSHIP

"How do you define leadership? I mean, leadership is a very strange word because, you know, some people have it, some people don't and nobody knows why. I mean, Winston Churchill was an unbelievable leader. Why? He was born with a speech impediment, he had all sorts of problems, he certainly wasn't a handsome man, and, yet, he was a great leader. Why was he a great leader? Nobody knows, he was a great leader."

## Source

"Transcript: Donald Trump announces plans to form presidential explor-atory committee," *Larry King Live*, CNN.com, October 8, 1999.
*www.cnn.com/ALLPOLITICS/stories/1999/10/08/trump.transcript/*

# MCCAIN, JOHN AS A WAR HERO

"He's not a war hero. He's a war hero because he was captured. I like people who weren't captured."

## Source

"John McCain Says Donald Trump's Remarks Will Hurt Him Among Veterans," by Alan Rappeport, FirstDraft, *New York Times*, July 20, 2015.
*www.nytimes.com/politics/first-draft/2015/07/20/john-mccain-says-donald-trumps-remarks-will-hurt-him-among-veterans/*

## In Context

In Iowa, at an event for social conservatives, Trump appeared to denigrate Senator John McCain, a former POW who was held by the North Vietnamese. Trump's comments drew fire from veterans, including McCain himself, who said, on MSNBC's *Morning Joe* program, "I think he may owe an apology to the families and those that have sacrificed in conflict and those who have undergone the prison experience in serving their country."

Trump responded, in a phone call to the *Today* television show, that he was pilloried by the media for a comment taken out of context. "I do also respect greatly people who aren't captured; nobody talks about them. We talk about John McCain, and I think it's great and he is a brave man and all of that, but we don't talk about people who weren't captured, and that is what I was trying to refer to."

## MERIT SYSTEM FOR IMMIGRANTS

"I'm a very big believer in the merit system. I have to tell you: Some of these people have been here, they've done a good job. You know, in some cases, sadly, they've been living under the shadows . . . If somebody's been outstanding, we try and work something out. But before we do anything, we have to secure the border because the border is like having no border."

### Source

"Donald Trump suggests 'merit system' for undocumented immigrants," by Brent Johnson, NJ.com, July 25, 2015.

*www.nj.com/politics/index.ssf/2015/07/donald_trump_hints_at_merit_system_for_undocumente.html*

### In Context

Trump has taken a lot of heat for his incendiary comments about illegal Mexican immigrants. But he tempered it with a final comment: "And some, I assume, are good people."

When he was asked to clarify his position, in an interview on Fox News (*Media Buzz*, July 5, 2015), he responded: "I don't mind apologizing for things. But I can't apologize for the truth. I said tremendous crime is coming across. Everybody knows that's true. And it's happening all the time. So, why, when I mention, all of a sudden I'm a racist. I'm not a racist. I don't have a racist bone in my body."

Trump contended that his comments were taken out of context.

# MURDER IN SAN FRANCISCO

"This man—or this animal—that shot the wonderful, that beautiful woman in San Francisco, this guy was pushed out by Mexico. We bring them back and they push them out. Mexico pushes back people across the border that are criminals, that are drug dealers. They're causing tremendous problems. In terms of crime, in terms of murder, in terms of rape . . . if somebody is an illegal immigrant they shouldn't be here at all. There shouldn't be any crime. They're not supposed to be in our country. And I'm not just talking Mexico . . . And when you say citizenship, the most we would be talking about was legal (status). But let me just tell you, before I even think about that, we have to build a . . . wall, a real wall. Not a wall that people walk through."

## Source

"Jan Brewer: Donald Trump 'Telling It Like It Really, Truly Is,'" by Susan Jones, CNSNews.com, July 9, 2015.

*www.cnsnews.com/news/article/susan-jones/jan-brewer-donald-trump-telling-it-it-really-truly*

## In Context

The "animal" to whom Trump referred is Juan Francisco Lopez-Sanchez, an illegal immigrant who has been deported five times. Sanchez, with four felony drug convictions and seventeen years in prison for illegal entry into the United States, is alleged to have shot Kathryn Steinle, a woman on a San Francisco pier. He claims he found a handgun wrapped up in a shirt on the pier, and it accidentally discharged when he picked it up. (The gun was traced back to a U.S. federal agent.) He has pled not guilty.

Arizona governor Jan Brewer praised Trump for bringing attention to the issue of illegal immigration. She told CNN's Don Lemon on July 8, 2015, "I believe Mr. Trump is kind of telling it like it really, truly is. You know, being the governor of (Arizona), the gateway of illegal immigration for six years, we had to deal with a lot of things. I think that the people of Arizona realize that we picked up the tab for the majority of the violence that comes across to our border with regards to the drug cartels, the smugglers, the drop houses. It has been horrendous. And, of course, they come through Arizona and therefore, end up in other states and go throughout the country."

# NUCLEAR WEAPONS

"I think we need massive protection and unfortunately, you know, nuclear is the protection. It's not just the question of having a million soldiers nowadays. You need the protection because North Korea has it . . . Iran is going to have it, Pakistan has it, India has it. Hopefully, India is on our side a little more than most but people are getting it and Russia has it big league and China has it, but you know, Putin said about a month ago and I was shocked to hear it— first time I've ever heard it from that kind of a power. Essentially he said don't mess with us, we have nuclear weapons. Do you remember that?"

## Source

"Donald Trump on Things 2016," by Hugh Hewitt, transcript, HughHewitt.com, August 3, 2015.

*www.hughhewitt.com/donald-trump-on-things-2016/*

## In Context

Trump told Newsmax that he opposes the deal the Obama administration made with Iran, regarding nuclear weapons. As Trump told reporters, "This deal sets off a nuclear arms race in the Middle East, which is the most unstable region in the world. It is a horrible and perhaps catastrophic event for Israel." (TeaParty.org, July 14, 2015.)

## OFFENDING HISPANICS

"Well, they shouldn't feel slighted. And what I said was right. This country is becoming a dumping ground for the entire world. The United States. We own $19 trillion. We're going to be up to $20 and $22 and $24 is a really magic number. That's a really bad number. That's, like, the point of no return.

"We can't afford this anymore. We have incompetent leaders. The president is incompetent. We have incompetent leaders and incompetent negotiators. Mexico, on the other hand, has very good negotiators. I'm pointing this out. I love the people of Mexico. I respect the people of Mexico. And I respect Mexico.

"But the fact is that if I were president, believe me, it wouldn't be the way it is right now. And I'll tell you this, I'd end up having a better relation with Mexico than the United States has right now. We would cherish each other. Right now there's tremendous animosity between the United States and Mexico, despite the fact that Mexico's making all the money. They're making all the money. We're getting killed. So I just finish by saying this. I really like Mexico and I love the people of Mexico. There's nothing else to say. If I were president, the United States would be an amazing place again."

### Source

"Transcript: Donald Trump Exclusive Telemundo Interview," by José Díaz-Balart, NBCUniversal MediaVillage, Noticiero Telemundo, June 25, 2015.

*https://www.nbcumv.com/news/transcript%C2%A0-donald-trump-exclusive-telemundo-interview*

# PAIN-CAPABLE UNBORN CHILD PROTECTION ACT

"I support the Pain-Capable Unborn Child Protection Act and urge Congress to pass this bill. A ban on elective abortions after twenty weeks will protect unborn children. We should not be one of seven countries that allows elective abortions after twenty weeks. It goes against our core values."

## Source

"Just In: *Brody File* Exclusive: Donald Trump Comes Out in Support of 20-Week Abortion Ban," by David Brody, CBN News, original airdate April, 2011.

*http://blogs.cbn.com/thebrodyfile/archive/2015/07/22/just-in-brody-file-exclusive-donald-trump-comes-out-in.aspx*

# PALIN, SARAH

"Well, I don't think she'd want to, because at the—the answer is—you know, I like Sarah Palin a lot. I think Sarah Palin has got very unfair press. I think the press has treated her very unfairly. But I would pick somebody that would be a terrific—you know, you have to view it as really who would be a good president in case something happened. But I would—there are many, many people out there that I think would be very good."

## Source

"*This Week* Transcript: Donald Trump," interview by Jonathan Karl, ABC News, August 2, 2015.

*http://abcnews.go.com/Politics/week-transcript-donald-trump/story?id=32829376*

### In Context

In May 2015, at a town hall meeting in Livingston, New Jersey, presidential candidate Gov. Chris Christie was asked if he'd consider Sarah Palin as a running mate. He replied, "Sure. I'd choose someone like Sarah Palin. There aren't many people who have as large a base as she's got. Judging from your reaction today—why not? In fact, I'd choose Sarah Palin."

Trump, though, is hedging his bets. Aware that the VP is only a heartbeat away from the presidency, Trump is chary of Palin as a choice, for reasons he didn't explain, though Palin's lackluster interview with Katie Couric in 2008 may have been a contributing factor.

On August 28, 2015, Palin interviewed Trump on One America News Network. The two celebrities showered one another with compliments. "If you look at what's happening with this country, it's so sad. You've pointed it out for years. I have to tell you you're a terrific person . . . One of the reasons I've always liked you, Sarah, you have that great connection [with veterans]," he told her.

## PLANNED PARENTHOOD

"I am against abortion . . . and that is a tremendous amount of work they do."

### Source

"Donald Trump Gets Womansplained on Planned Parenthood," by Nina Bahadur, HuffingtonPost.com, September 10, 2015, quoting from *The View*, with Whoopi Goldberg explaining, "Planned Parenthood does abortions for 3 percent of the people who come to them. The rest is women's health. And that percent is not federally funded, so nobody's tax money is being used for abortions. And yet if you defund Planned Parenthood, millions of women will not get healthcare. I think, since you've shown to have such a big heart for the Syrians, you might wanna extend that to women in this country."

*www.huffingtonpost.com/2015/09/10/donald-trump-gets-womansplained-on-planned-parenthood_n_8118150.html*

### In Context

Planned Parenthood's annual report for 2013–2014 states that abortion services comprise 3 percent of their services; 42 percent is for sexually transmitted diseases testing and treatment, 34 percent for contraception, 9 percent for cancer screening and prevention; 11 percent for other women's health services, and 1 percent for other services.

## POLITICIANS' IMPOTENCE

"So I've watched the politicians. I've dealt with them all my life. If you can't make a good deal with a politician, then there's something wrong with you. You're certainly not very good. And that's what we have representing us. They will never make America great again. They don't even have a chance. They're controlled fully—they're controlled fully by the lobbyists, by the donors, and by the special interests, fully."

### Source

"Donald Trump Transcript: 'Our Country Needs a Truly Great Leader,'" by Federal News Service, *Wall Street Journal*, June 16, 2015.

*http://blogs.wsj.com/washwire/2015/06/16/donald-trump-transcript-our-country-needs-a-truly-great-leader/*

### In Context

Trump's trump card, so to speak, is that he's not representative of politics as usual—especially not candidates running for presidential office. The tried-and-true methods of fundraising, says Trump, result in politicians who have been bought as a result of campaign contributions, who in turn will dispense political favors after being installed in high political office. Trump's wealth allows him the luxury of not having to depend on contributions to fund his campaign; therefore, he is not beholden to anyone, or any special interest groups. So political cronyism will not be an issue with him, as it is for all the other candidates for the presidency.

# PRESIDENT OBAMA'S LACK OF LEADERSHIP

"You really need leadership. You have to get people into a room and get something that is good for everybody whether its compromise or whatever but you have to get them into a room and you have to lead and that hasn't happened under President Obama."

### Source

"Donald Trump: 'I pay as little as possible' in taxes," by Rebecca Kaplan, *Face the Nation*, CBS News, August 2, 2015.

*www.cbsnews.com/news/donald-trump-i-pay-as-little-as-possible-in-taxes/*

### In Context

Trump is not an Obama fan. As he told Jonathan Karl of ABC News' *This Week* (August 2, 2015), "I think he has done a very poor job as president. We have $18 trillion right now in debt and going up rapidly . . . Because I think he has set a very poor standard. I think he has set a low bar and I think it's a shame for the African-American people. And by the way, he has done nothing for African-Americans. You look at what's going on with their income levels. You look at what's gone on with their youth. I thought that he would be a great cheerleader for this country. I thought he'd do a fabulous job for the African-American citizens of this country." ("*This Week* Transcript: Donald Trump," interview by Jonathan Karl, ABC News, 2015.)

PolitiFact.com (August 2, 2015) after examining the facts, concluded that "Trump is wrong by several important measures" and stated that "Trump said that under Obama, income levels and unemployment numbers 'are worse now than just about ever' for African-Americans. Some key statistics for African-Americans, such as unemployment, improved significantly during Obama's tenure. The ones that stagnated or worsened under Obama are still relatively positive compared to recent history.

"We rate the claim false."

## PRESIDENTIAL BID

*When asked: "Do you see your bid as similar to Ross Perot's 1992 maverick presidential campaign?"* "No. I don't consider Perot a movement. This is a movement. It's a different movement than I think you've ever seen before. Angry, sad, disappointed, devastated by what's happened to the country. Mourning. Some of these people who've lost their kids to [illegal immigrants], it's mourning. I spoke to one of the mothers today who came to see me, lost her son five years ago. It was like it was yesterday. Their lives are [expletive] over. She'll never be happy.

"The campaign is about making America great again."

## Source

"Listening to Donald Trump swear and talk politics on his private plane," by Robert Costa, *Washington Post*, July 12, 2015.

*www.washingtonpost.com/news/post-politics/wp/2015/07/12/listening-to-donald-trump-swear-and-talk-politics-on-his-private-plane/*

## In Context

James Surowiecki of the *New Yorker* ("Donald Trump's Sales Pitch," August 10, 2015) summed it up: "You could not ask for a better illustration of the complexity of ordinary Americans' attitudes toward class, wealth, and social identity than the fact that a billionaire's popularity among working-class voters has given him the lead in the race for the Republican presidential nomination. In a recent *Washington Post*/ABC poll, Trump was the candidate of choice of a full third of white Republicans with no college education."

# PUBLIC PERCEPTION

"I think that people see me as somebody that loves the country. But maybe even more importantly will not let our great country be ripped off by so many others. Everybody is ripping us. And I think they see that. They think I'm a smart guy. They think I have done well in all of that. But maybe above all, they see a person that loves this country, is passionate about this country and will not let China and OPEC and these people take advantage of us any longer. I will tell you, if oil goes up any higher, this country will have a major, major economic collapse. We cannot afford it. We cannot allow it to happen. And I think they see me as a smart, tough guy."

## Source

"Donald Trump Interview: Transcript Part Two," by George Stephanopoulos, ABC News, April 19, 2011.

*http://blogs.abcnews.com/george/2011/04/donald-trump-interview-transcript-part-two.html*

## In Context

Trump has traction with blue-collar Americans because he strikes a responsive chord when he talks about standing up to the Chinese in foreign trade deals and putting Americans back on the job. Jerry Hubbard, a retiree who lives in Flint, Michigan, and who has seen the devastating erosion of U.S. auto jobs in town, said: "I worked at Plant 36. It's all gone. It's all limestone. You can't rape a place like that. General Motors jobs made this place . . . A lot of what he says hit a chord with me. Immigration and jobs going to China—this area's really suffered from that. I just like somebody that stands up for what he speaks about." ("Why Donald Trump makes sense to many voters—even some Democrats," by David Weigel, *Washington Post*, August 15, 2015.)

# PUBLIC SKEPTICISM

"First, people said I would never run, and I did. Then, they said, I would never file my statement of candidacy with the FEC, and I did. Next, they said I would never file my personal financial disclosure forms. I filed them early despite the fact that I am allowed two 45-day [sic] extensions . . . Now I have surged in the polls and am fighting to Make America Great Again. I look forward to the challenge of winning the presidency and doing a fantastic job for our country. I will make the United States rich and strong and respected again, but also a country with a 'big heart' toward the care of our people."

## Source

"Donald Trump's Team Says His 'Massive' Net Worth is More Than 'TEN BILLION DOLLARS,'" by Igor Bobic, HuffPost Politics, HuffingtonPost .com, July 15, 2015.

*www.huffingtonpost.com/entry/donald-trump-net-worth_55a6a342e 4b0c5f0322c1726*

## In Context

Trump's recurring interest in a bid to be the POTUS (president of the United States) began in 1988, when a GOP activist named Mike Dunbar started a Draft Trump movement, because, as he told the Associated Press, "I figure Trump has what it takes." Though Trump discounted that he was running, he did travel in October 1987 to New Hampshire, where he made political comments. He later acknowledged that event germinated his interest in presidential politics because it "planted the seed." For the 2000 presidential race, Trump told the *New York Times,* "It's a very great possibility that I will run." He'd run, he said, under New York's Independence Party. Months after that announcement, however, he pulled out, stating that he couldn't win as an Independent.

The media reported that he flirted with the possibility of running in 2006, but in 2012, Trump garnered a lot of press attention by attacking President Obama, and stated he wanted to go mano a mano with him to blunt the president's re-election bid. But, once again, he begged off.

Not surprisingly, for the 2016 presidential bid, voters felt that it might be another case of a Trump head fake. However, this time he took the decisive step of declaring his candidacy.

In his 1990 book *Trump: Surviving at the Top*, he downplays any interest in public service, asserting, "I'm not a politician. I wouldn't want to get involved in the compromises, the glad-handing, and all the other demeaning things you have to do to get votes."

The times have changed, though, and so did Trump's mind about running for the highest political office in the land.

## THE REPUBLICAN NATIONAL COMMITTEE

"The RNC has not been supportive. They were always supportive when I was a contributor. I was their fair-haired boy . . . The RNC has been, I think, very foolish . . . I'm not in the gang. I'm not in the group where the group does whatever it's supposed to do. I want to do what's right for the country—not what's good for special interest groups that contribute, not what's good for the lobbyists and the donors."

### Source

"Exclusive: Trump threatens third-party run," by Kevin Cirilli and Bob Cusack, TheHill.com, July 23, 2015.

*http://thehill.com/homenews/campaign/248910-exclusive-trump-threatens-third-party-run*

### In Context

Given its druthers, the RNC would prefer that Trump not run, because he's taking all the oxygen out of the room. By virtue of leading in the polls, Trump was center stage at the first three Republican debates, flanked by the other candidates. As the *Washington Post* ("As Republicans ready to debate . . . ," August

5, 2015), put it: "At the moment, Trump's catapulting candidacy is the dominant story line. One of the debate moderators, Chris Wallace, said Tuesday evening on Fox, 'We don't want to make it the Donald Trump show, but it is.'"

## RUNNING AS AN INDEPENDENT

"I cannot say if I'm the nominee, I will pledge I will not run as an independent. But—and I am discussing it with everybody, but I'm, you know, talking a lot of leverage . . . I want to win as a Republican. I want to run as the Republican nominee."

### Source
"The 10 lines that capture the 10 candidates' key moments," and "Trump was clear about his (lack of) loyalty to the GOP," by Kathleen Hennessey, Trail Guide: Campaign 2016, *Los Angeles Times*, August 6, 2015.

### In Context
Even before the highly anticipated first Republican debate, it was clear that its first salvo was designed to put Trump on the spot by forcing him to answer a question that assuredly would garner boos from the audience comprised of hardcore Republicans.

Trump made it clear that he wanted to run on the Republican ticket, but he also wanted to make it just as clear that he wanted to keep his options open and, if necessary, run as a third-party candidate, regardless of the impact on the Republican Party. However, on September 3, he signed a pledge not to do so. Time will tell whether he chooses to honor that pledge, which is not legally binding.

# SAUDI ARABIA

*Trump:* "I have people. I can send two people into a room. One person comes home with the bacon, the other one doesn't. Same, same thing. We protect Saudi Arabia. We have soldiers over there, that they don't pay us for, by the way. We have soldiers, all over the Middle East, protecting these countries. If we withdraw, look at what happened with Kuwait. We went back, we took it over, we handed it back to these characters. We hand—and now they won't invest in the United States, because their return on investment isn't good enough. It's all about the way it's said. We have soldiers over there. We protect them. If we're not there, it would fall. It may fall anyway."

*George Stephanopoulos:* "So, you would threaten to take away that protection?"

*Trump:* "Oh, absolutely. Absolutely. Lets—let me tell you something. Oil prices might go down. Because there's plenty of oil, all over the world. Ships at sea. They don't know where to dump it. I saw a report yesterday. There's so much oil, all over the world, they don't know where to dump it. And Saudi Arabia says, 'Oh, there's too much oil.' . . . Did you see the report? They want to reduce oil production. Do you think they're our friends? They're not our friends."

## Source

"Donald Trump Interview: Transcript Part One," by George Stephanopoulos, ABC News, April 19, 2011.

*http://blogs.abcnews.com/george/2011/04/donald-trump-interview-transcript-part-one.html*

# SECOND AMENDMENT

"It is so important that we maintain the Second Amendment and that we maintain it strongly. And one of the main reasons is because the good people, the upstanding people, follow laws and norms but the bad ones don't. So if the Second Amendment weren't there to protect our rights and someone tampered with them, the good people would be affected but the bad people wouldn't care—they couldn't care less.

"Paris has virtually the most restrictive laws that exist anywhere, and you look at the slaughter at *Charlie Hebdo*, and that's what it was—it was a slaughter in which the people never had a chance. And I made the statement then that if people had guns in that room the outcome would have been a hell-of-a-lot better than it ended up being, where they were just slaughtered at will."

## Source

"Exclusive—Donald Trump: We Must Maintain 2nd Amendment 'In Its Strongest Form,'" by A.W.R. Hawkins, Breitbart News, April 11, 2015.

*www.breitbart.com/big-government/2015/04/11/exclusive-donald-trump-we-must-maintain-2nd-amendment-in-its-strongest-form/*

## In Context

A satirical magazine, *Charlie Hebdo* (trans.: *Charlie Weekly*), based in Paris, France, was the locus for an attack by terrorists—not once but three times: in 2011, 2012, and 2015, ostensibly because of perceived blasphemous cartoons mocking the prophet Muhammad. The third attack resulted in the killing of twelve people.

In the wake of that attack, the print run of the magazine mushroomed from 60,000 copies (its usual run) to 5 million, with all proceeds going to the affected families.

Afterward, the editor/publisher of the magazine, Laurent Sourisseau, said it will no longer publish cartoons satirizing Muhammad. It's an affront to the Muslim religion and a catalyst for terrorists, especially for al-Qaeda's Yemen branch that claimed responsibility for the attack.

## SELF-FINANCING

"I am not a politician. I can't be bought. I won't be running around the country begging people for money for my campaign. I won't owe anybody anything. I won't be beholden to anyone except to you, the American people, if you elect me to serve as your president."

### Source
"Donald J. Trump Presidential Announcement As Delivered at Trump Tower in New York City on June 16, 2015." [Note: This was the original document intended to be read, but instead was used as a talking outline for his announcement.]

*http://blog.4president.org/2016/2015/06/donald-j-trump-presidential-announcement-speech-as-delivered-at-trump-tower-in-new-york-city-on-june.html*

### In Context
Unlike all the other candidates—Republican, Democrat, or independent—Trump is self-financing his campaign because he can. Though estimates of his net worth vary, there's no question that he's the richest candidate—a

billionaire who can write his own checks instead of relying on outside financial help.

It gives Trump a huge tactical advantage over the other candidates who are running against him.

Trump, despite his wealth, feels that he's in touch with the man on the street. In *Trump: Surviving at the Top*, he writes: "As I walk along [the streets of New York City], about twenty-five perfect strangers wave and shout, 'Hi, Donald,' and 'How're you doing, Donald,' and 'Keep up the good work.' One thing this proves to me is that the average working man or woman is a lot better adjusted and more secure than the supposedly successful people who stare down at them from the penthouses."

## SELF-PROMOTION

*When asked, "[S]ome people say you troll the Republican Party to promote your various shows, buildings, golf courses. How do you respond to that?"*

"Well, it's not. Look, I'm a Republican. I'm a very conservative guy in many respects, I guess, in most respects. But I'm so disappointed, and many of the Republicans have come up to my office. [Scott] Walker just left, and you know, all good guys. I mean, they're up here and they want support, and they want a lot of other things. Who know what they want? But they do come up and they do respect my audience, because I have a big audience. As you know, I have many millions of people on Facebook and Twitter and all of this. But I don't do, I am so disappointed that whether it's Benghazi or whether it's so many other subjects—IRS, so many subjects, whether it's having to do with whether it's Hillary or the president, it's all talk and it's no action. They start off, they're going to go after it, and that's the last you ever hear of it."

## Source

"Donald Trump on 2016 and Trolling the GOP," by Hugh Hewitt, transcript, HughHewitt.com, February 25, 2015.

*www.hughhewitt.com/donald-trump-on-2016-and-trolling-the-gop/*

# SNOWDEN, EDWARD

"You know, spies in the old days used to be executed. This guy is becoming a hero in some circles. Now, I will say, with the passage of time, even people that were sort of liking him and were trying to go on his side are maybe dropping out . . . We have to get him back and we have to get him back fast. It could take months or it could take years, and that would be pathetic. This guy's a bad guy and, you know, there's still a thing called execution . . . You have thousands of people with access to material like this. We're not going to have a country any longer."

## Source

"Donald Trump: NSA Whistleblower Snowden Should Be 'Assassinated,'" by Kristin Tate, MrConservative.com, not dated.

*http://mrconservative.com/2013/06/20087-donald-trump-nsa-whistleblower-snowden-should-be-assassinated/*

## In Context

Trump's position: no mercy to traitors. In an interview with *Fox & Friends*, cited by Tal Kopan for Politico.com ("Trump: Snowden 'really hurt us,'" June 24, 2013), Trump said that Snowden is "a terrible guy who's really set our country back . . . He's revealing things that nobody thought possible, and I think he's probably got stuff that's far—that's maybe why he's staying in Russia. Russia's very smart, and they're probably getting every possible thing out of him. They say, 'Hey wait a minute, let's not send him to Ecuador or wherever he's going. Let's immediately—let's talk to him for a couple more days. This is good stuff.'"

## SOUTH KOREA

"And then we defend South Korea? . . . And then we send the great aircraft carrier, the USS *George Washington*, and destroyers to defend South Korea. They don't pay us? They don't pay us for it. We send all these ships, hundreds of millions of dollars to protect South Korea from North Korea . . . We have thou—you know, we have what? 20,000–25,000 soldiers over there. They don't even pay us for this. What are we doing? What are we thinking? What are we thinking? . . .

"I say I can't get bids from American companies, because China manipulates their currency and they can't compete with Chinese companies . . . I said, 'Does anybody make televisions in the United States?' You know what the answer was. We can't find anybody. They're all from China, from Japan, from South Korea. And I said to 'em, because I bought thousands of them."

### Source

"Donald Trump Interview: Transcript Part Two," by George Stephanopoulos, ABC News, April 19, 2011.

*http://blogs.abcnews.com/george/2011/04/donald-trump-interview-transcript-part-two.html*

# A SUCCESSFUL CANDIDATE

"The politicians—and I know all of them—they're never going to make this country great . . . I'm the most successful person ever to run for the presidency, by far. Nobody's ever been more successful than me. I'm the most successful person ever to run. Ross Perot isn't successful like me. Romney—I have a Gucci store that's worth more than Romney."

### Source

"Trump: I won't do Iowa Straw Poll if everyone backs out," by Josh Hafner, *Des Moines Register*, June 2, 2015.

*www.desmoinesregister.com/story/news/elections/presidential/caucus/2015/06/01/donald-trump-straw-poll-mitt-romney-gucci-store/28313569/*

# TAXES

"Well, I think the thing about the flat tax, I know it very well. What I don't like is that if you make $200 million a year, you pay 10 percent, you're paying very little relatively to somebody that's making $50,000 a year and has to hire H&R Block to do the [tax preparation]—because it's so complicated.

"One thing I'll say to [presidential candidate] Ben [Carson] is that we've had a graduated tax system for many years, so it's not a socialistic thing. What I'd like to do, and I'll be putting in the plan in about two weeks, and I think people are going to like it, it's a major reduction in taxes. It's a major reduction for the middle class. The hedge fund guys won't like me as much as they like me right now. I know them all, but they'll pay more.

"I know people that are making a tremendous amount of money and paying virtually no tax, and I think it's unfair."

## Source

"Transcript: Read the Full Text of the Second Republican Debate," by Ryan Teague Beckwith, Time.com, September 16, 2015.

*http://time.com/4037239/second-republican-debate-transcript-cnn/*

## In Context

On September 28, 2015, the Trump campaign released the candidate's tax plan. Trump proposes that those earning $25,000 and below ($50,000 for couples) pay no tax. The highest individual tax rate would be 25 percent (the current highest rate is 39.6 percent). In addition, business tax rates would be cut to 15 percent and overseas earnings would be taxed only once. The plan eliminates an important tax loophole for hedge fund managers but maintains it for private equity earners. Concerning the plan, Trump said, "My plan will bring sanity, common sense and simplification to our country's catastrophic tax code. It will create jobs and incentives of all kinds while simultaneously growing the economy." ("Trump Plan Cuts Taxes for Millions," by Monica Langley and John D. McKinnon, *Wall Street Journal*, September 29, 2015, *www.wsj.com/articles/trump-plan-cuts-taxes-for-millions-1443427200.*)

# TRUMPING THE OTHER CANDIDATES

*When asked: "Why are you the last one [the DNC] wants to see in the race?"*

"Because they think I would be most effective in beating Hillary Clinton. Because I know what it takes to win. I know how to win. Mitt Romney did not know how to win. Mitt Romney choked. Mitt Romney did a poor job of closing. Mitt Romney disappeared a month before the election."

## Source

"Donald Trump Interview: 'I Don't Want to Be Disruptive,'" by Heather Haddon, *Wall Street Journal*, June 19, 2015.

*http://blogs.wsj.com/washwire/2015/06/19/donald-trump-interview-i-dont-want-to-be-disruptive/*

# VACCINATIONS AND AUTISM

*When asked, "You wrote massive combined inoculations to small children is the cause for a big increase in autism. Spread shots over a long period, and watch positive result. Do you stand by that, Donald Trump?"*

"Okay, I do, and let me explain it real quickly. I am a total believer in getting the shots and having it done, and I am a total believer, 100 percent, nobody a bigger believer. What I don't like seeing is that 20-pound little baby going in and having this one massive inoculation with all of these things combined. I'd like it spread over, because look, our autism rate is at a level that it's never been. Nobody's ever, you know, in the old days, you didn't even hear about autism, and now it's at a level that's so high, especially in boys, but so high that nobody can even believe it. What I'm saying is 100 percent I want to see it happen. I want everybody, but it should be spread over. Smaller doses over a longer period of time. So spread it out over a year. There's no harm in that, and I believe autism will go way down."

## Source

"Donald Trump on 2016 and Trolling the GOP," by Hugh Hewitt, transcript, HughHewitt.com, February 25, 2015.

*www.hughhewitt.com/donald-trump-on-2016-and-trolling-the-gop/*

## In Context

The Centers for Disease Control and Prevention (CDC) states on its website, "Some people have had concerns that ASD might be linked to the vaccines children receive, but studies have shown that there is no link between receiving vaccines and developing ASD . . . A 2013 CDC study added to the research showing that vaccines do not cause ASD. The study looked at the number of antigens . . . from vaccines during the first two years of life. The results showed that the total amount of antigen from vaccines received was the same between children with ASD and those that did not have ASD. ("Vaccines Do Not Cause Autism," CDC Statement: 2004 Pediatrics Paper on MMR and Autism, CDC.gov.)

# VETERANS

"You look at what's happening with the veterans. The veterans are being treated like third-class citizens. It's horrible what's going on and John McCain is so involved with the veterans, but nothing happens because they're politicians ultimately."

## Source

"Trump Interview: 'Admire Palin,' Political Media 'Amazingly Dishonest,' Real Climate Change 'Nuclear,'" by Michelle Moons, Breitbart News, July 27, 2015.

*www.breitbart.com/big-government/2015/07/27/trump-interview-admire-palin-political-media-amazingly-dishonest-real-climate-change-nuclear/*

### In Context

When Trump made a comment about Senator John McCain not being a war hero, it sparked off a war of words in the media. Trump, who attended a military academy prep school, never served in the U.S. military, but some say he served its veterans well, as Vincent McGowan (New York's Vietnam Veterans Plaza) pointed out in a story from ABCNews.go.com ("Leader of New York Veterans Group Defends Donald Trump," by John Santucci, July 20, 2015). McGowan explained that when the construction of the Veterans Plaza stalled, Trump set up a matching fund, with $1 million, that was instrumental in completing its construction.

The organization also turned to Trump in 1995 to support a veteran's parade. Trump donated $175,000 to the cause, and offered the use of his helicopter to ferry staffers within the city, reported ABCNews.go.com. Also, "McGowan recalled a particular experience a few years back, a staff sergeant had just retired after ten years of service, wanted to see New York but was down on his luck. McGowan called Trump, who gave the veteran a tour of Trump Tower, took him to lunch, and then handed him a check for $10,000 to jump-start his education."

# VETERAN CARE AND SENATOR JOHN MCCAIN

"I believe that I will do far more for veterans than John McCain has done for many, many years, with all talk, no action. He's on television all the time, talking, talking. Nothing gets done. You look at what's happening to our veterans—they're being decimated, OK. So I will do far more for veterans than anybody. I'll be able to build them new hospitals, I'll be able to build them care centers. I'll be able to help the veterans.

"John McCain has failed. Because all you have to do is take a look—what you report on all the time, take a look at the scandal at the Veterans' Administration and the disastrous conditions under which our veterans have to live. And believe me, I built, with a small group, the Vietnam memorial in downtown Manhattan. I know what it is to help people and I know what it is to help veterans."

### Source

*"This Week* Transcript: Donald Trump," interview by Martha Raddatz, ABC News, July 19, 2015.

*http://abcnews.go.com/Politics/week-transcript-donald-trump/story?id=32528691*

## WATERBOARDING

"I would be inclined to be very strong. When people are chopping off other people's heads and then we're worried about waterboarding and we can't, because I have no doubt that that works. I have absolutely no doubt."

### Source

*"This Week* Transcript: Donald Trump," interview by Jonathan Karl, ABC News, August 2, 2015.

*http://abcnews.go.com/Politics/week-transcript-donald-trump/story?id=32829376*

### In Context

"Waterboarding has been around for centuries. It was a common interrogation technique during the Italian Inquisition of the 1500s and was used perhaps most famously in Cambodian prisons during the reign of the Khmer Rouge regime during the 1970s. As late as November 2005, waterboarding was on the CIA's list of approved 'enhanced interrogation techniques' intended for use against high-value terror suspects. And according to memos released by the U.S. Department of Justice in April 2009, waterboarding was among ten torture techniques authorized for the interrogation of an al-Qaeda operative. In a nutshell, waterboarding makes a person feel like he is drowning." ("What is waterboarding?," by Julia Layton, HowStuffWorks.com, *http://science.howstuffworks.com/water-boarding.htm.*)

Trump's position on dealing with ISIS operatives closely resembles a law code dating back to a Mesopotamian king Hammurabi (1792–1750 B.C.E.). The prologue to the list of 282 draconian laws states that he wanted "to make justice visible in the land, to destroy the wicked person and the evil-doer, that the strong might not injure the weak." From Hammurabi's code we get the popular expression "an eye for an eye, a tooth for a tooth," which sets up a moral equivalency of justice based on social status—commoners didn't suffer the same harsh fate as those in the upper class.

## WHAT PEOPLE WANT

"Well, I think that, more than anything else, they want to see us become great again. It's my theme, my whole theme is, 'Make America Great Again.' It's a concept of greatness for this country. They are tired of being ripped off by every single country that does business with us. Whether it's China, Japan, Mexico, Vietnam—which is in there big and heavy right now—Japan with the cars. And you know, the one-way street. They're tired of looking at what happens, they are tired of us having our . . . let's say finest and brightest not being involved in the most important decisions, and being someplace else. They want to see great trade deals, they want to see a strong military. They want to see reduced debt, because we are at a point where we are going to be soon at $19 trillion and they just, you know, they can't stand seeing it. They want to see our veterans taken care of, because they are not, they are being absolutely mistreated. There are many things they want to see. There are many points of anger in this country."

### Source

"*The Economist* interviews Donald Trump," staff interviewer, Economist .com, from the print edition, September 3, 2015.

*www.economist.com/news/briefing/21663216-donald-trump-has-become-surprise-republican-frontrunner-early-2016-us-presidential*

# Trump on Business

## ADVICE TO ENTREPRENEURS

"You have to love what you do. Without passion, great success is hard to come by. An entrepreneur will have tough times if he or she isn't passionate about what they're doing. People who love what they're doing don't give up. It's never even a consideration. It's a pretty simple formula."

### Source
"Ten Questions with Donald Trump," by Guy Kawasaki, GuyKawasaki .com, January 25, 2007.

*http://guykawasaki.com/ten_questions_w-5/*

## THE ART OF THE DEAL

*To George Stephanopoulos:* "I've had very few failures, George. And if I do have a failure, I try and make it a success. For instance, if a market collapses in the midst of a big construction job, which I've had happen a number of times, in some cases, I've made those jobs more successful.

"I go back to the banks. I fight with them. I negotiate. I do all sorts of things. And I've had deals that should have been disasters and would have been for most people and they've become great successes, actually more successful than if the market had stayed good.

"But I would say this more than anything else, you have to learn from tough times. And I've learned a lot."

### Source

"*This Week* Transcript: Donald Trump," interview by George Stephanopoulos, ABC News, August 23, 2015.

*http://abcnews.go.com/Politics/week-transcript-donald-trump/story?id=33203713*

# ASPIRATIONS

"I like the challenge and tell the story of the coal miner's son. The coal miner gets black lung disease, his son gets it, then his son. If I had been the son of a coal miner, I would have left the damn mines. But most people don't have the imagination—or whatever—to leave their mine. They don't have 'it.'"

### Source

"Donald Trump," by Glenn Plaskin, *Playboy,* March 1990.

### In Context

Donald's father Fred spent his lifetime building low-cost buildings outside of Manhattan, but early on, Donald made it clear to his father that he wasn't interested in following his father's footsteps; instead, he wanted to put on his big league walking boots and stride across the East River separating the South Side from Manhattan, where he set his sights high, to its towering skyscrapers. There's no question that The Donald has imprinted his name in big letters on major buildings in New York City. His father was a successful millionaire, but the son became a successful billionaire.

"But if I had an edge over my father, it might have been in concepts—the concept of a building. It also might have been in scope. I would rather sell apartments to billionaires who want to live on Fifth Avenue and 57th Street than sell apartments to people in Brooklyn who are wonderful people but are going to chisel me down because every penny is important . . . I used to stand on the other side of the East River and look at Manhattan." ("Playboy Interview: Donald Trump," by David Hochman, *Playboy*, October 2004.)

## BANKRUPTCY

"Well, in the early nineties, I was in a lot of trouble because the real estate markets had collapsed; many of my friends went bankrupt, never to be heard from again. I never went bankrupt, but I was in deep trouble and now my company is much bigger, much stronger than it ever was before. So I don't view myself as 'comeback.' But when I speak, I have thousands of people come listen to speeches on success and everything else. Had I had a simple, smooth life, those crowds wouldn't exist."

### Source
"Donald Trump: The interview," by Gaby Wood, TheGuardian.com, January 7, 2007.

*www.theguardian.com/business/2007/jan/07/media.citynews*

## In Context

Trump has never personally declared bankruptcy and thus tells the media that he's never gone bankrupt. The Law Dictionary's James Hirby would agree—up to a point: "Trump himself has never filed for bankruptcy. His corporations have filed Chapter 11 bankruptcy four times . . . By filing for Chapter 11 bankruptcy, the corporation is allowed to continue running while restructuring and reducing its debt. By allowing the business to continue, employees still have their jobs and the business is still making money. Corporate debts still need to be repaid but they may be reduced. The corporation must develop a repayment plan and corporate budget. Both must be approved by the creditors and by the bankruptcy court."

Hirby cites the four corporate bankruptcies: in 1991, the Trump Taj Mahal; in 1992, the Trump Plaza Hotel in Atlantic City; in 2004, Trump Hotels and Casino Resorts; and in 2009, Trump Entertainment Resorts. (Fact checked by The Law Dictionary staff, for TheLawDictionary.org.)

As Trump himself told *Playboy* magazine in an October 2004 interview, "In the early 1990s I was highly leveraged when the real estate market collapsed. I'd borrowed a lot and had lots of debt . . . The hardest I've ever worked in my life was the period from 1990 to 1994, but my business is now bigger and stronger than ever before. I wouldn't want to do it again, but I learned that the world can change on the head of a dime, and that keeps things in perspective."

In Chapter 1 of *Trump: The Art of the Comeback*, the billionaire lays it all out for his readers, explaining that there were front-page stories that ran on March 26, 1991, in both the *New York Times* and the *Wall Street Journal* that were "predicting my demise, detailing the financial trouble I was in. Anybody with a brain who read those stories would have said I was finished. The stories were picked up by radio and television and blasted throughout the world. This was by far the worst moment of my life."

Trump, at that point, owed the banks nearly $1 billion because he had given his personal guarantee to secure loans that totaled $3.7 billion. In *Trump: The Art of the Comeback*, he describes the following incident: "One day, while walking down Fifth Avenue, hand in hand with Marla [Maples], I pointed across the street to a man holding a cup and with a seeing eye dog. I asked, 'Do you know who that is?'

"Marla said to me: 'Yes, Donald. He's a beggar. Isn't it too bad? He looks so sad!'

"I said, 'You're right. He's a beggar, but he's worth about $900 million more than me.'

"She looked at me and said, 'What do you mean, Donald? How could he possibly be worth $900 million more than you?'

"I said, 'Let's assume he's worth nothing (only from the standpoint of dollars)—I'm worth minus $900 million.'"

## BECOMING RICH

"Some people aren't meant to be rich . . . It's just something you have, something you're born with. Many people don't have the ability to be rich, because they're too lazy or they don't have the desire or the stick-to-itiveness. It's a talent. Some people have a talent for piano. Some people have a talent for raising a family. Some people have a talent for golf. I just happen to have a talent for making money."

### Source
"Playboy Interview: Donald Trump," by David Hochman, *Playboy*, October 2004.

## BRANDING BUILDINGS

"I mean, I put my name on buildings because it sells better. I don't do it because, gee, I need that. I mean, I get more per square foot in New York than anybody else by far. If you build a building here, and I build a building there . . . I will get substantially more per square foot . . . Now, it's not almost the same building. I build a better building. I use better finishes. It's just a better product. But I get more than other people. So when I put my name on it, people say: Oh, gee, he put his name on it."

### Source
"Transcript: Donald Trump announces plans to form presidential exploratory committee," *Larry King Live*, CNN.com, October 8, 1999.
*www.cnn.com/ALLPOLITICS/stories/1999/10/08/trump.transcript/*

## BUSINESS OPPORTUNITIES

"My theory is that there are always opportunities. They may be more difficult to find, but they are there. Research is important and one needs to be wary. However, I'm a cautious optimist and I think it's best to focus on the solution instead of the problem. The current economy is undoubtedly difficult but to focus solely on the difficulties is not a good solution or approach. It's also a great time to become innovative—that's what's needed. My strategy is to be on the lookout for opportunities. They're there."

### Source
"The Monday Interview with Donald Trump and Robert Kiyosaki," by Dick Donahue, PublishersWeekly.com, October 3, 2011.

*www.publishersweekly.com/pw/by-topic/authors/interviews/article/48931-the-monday-interview-with-donald-trump-and-robert-kiyosaki.html*

## BUSINESSMAN AS PRESIDENT

"Well, I'm tired of politicians being president, because I see the lousy job they do, and I'm just tired of it. And I think a lot of other people are. And, you know, you can do a great job as a businessman, nothing wrong with it. If Jack Welch, who runs General Electric brilliantly for twenty-two years, I mean, he should be a president, he should be president; he's great. Now, he wouldn't run, he wouldn't want to run. But, he's a brilliant man who has done an amazing job. He would be a fantastic president."

### Source

"Transcript: Donald Trump announces plans to form presidential exploratory committee," *Larry King Live*, CNN.com, October 8, 1999.

*www.cnn.com/ALLPOLITICS/stories/1999/10/08/trump.transcript/*

## DISLOYALTY

*In a* Vanity Fair *profile (September 1990), Marie Brenner told Trump that one of his lawyers told her, "Donald is a believer in the big-lie theory. If you say something again and again, people will believe you."* "One of my lawyers said that? I think if one of my lawyers said that, I'd like to know who he is, because I'd fire his ass. I'd like to find out who the scumbag is!"

## Source

"After the Gold Rush," by Marie Brenner, *Vanity Fair*, September 1990.

## In Context

During a Q&A with Trump, in front of 3,500 people at Starkey Hearing Technologies' Hearing Innovation Expo, Brandon Sawalich, the company's senior vice president, said, "We covered many topics, but one thing Trump said especially stood out to me. When I asked him what he values in an employee, he had a one-word answer: loyalty.

"To be honest, that wasn't the answer I was expecting from a man known for his ruthless business demeanor. I thought he would mention results, tenacity or fight. I wouldn't have been surprised if he had said something along those lines. But 'loyalty' hadn't crossed my mind.

"I've thought a lot about his answer since then. Loyalty may be considered a soft trait, but it shouldn't be. It's a sign that your business is doing something right, that what you stand for and how you operate resonates with your employees. A company that loses a once-loyal employee needs to examine what went wrong—and fast." ("3 lessons about loyalty that I learned from Donald Trump," by Brandon Sawalich, The Business Journals, February 2, 2015, *www.bizjournals.com/bizjournals/how-to/growth-strategies/2015/02/3-loyalty-lessons-learned-from-donald-trump.html.*)

In *Think Big and Kick Ass in Business and Life*, Trump tells the tale of a woman he mentored who previously worked in government. "I gave her a great job at the Trump Organization, and over time she became powerful in real estate. She bought a beautiful home."

"I needed her help," he wrote, during the early 1990s, when he was going through "tough times" and asked her to call a banker she knew that he was dealing with. She refused. He wrote her off permanently. Her business career and personal life later crashed.

"She ended up losing her home. Her husband, who was only in it for the money, walked out on her, and I was glad. Over the years many people have called asking for a recommendation for her. I only give her bad recommendations. I just can't stomach the disloyalty."

Trump's viewpoint is that if you help someone and that person, later in life, is in a position to respond in kind, to not offer assistance is a sign of disloyalty. In such an instance, he doesn't simply ignore the person—he wants his pound of flesh. "This woman was very disloyal, and now I go out of my way to make her life miserable. She calls asking to get together for lunch or for dinner. I never return her calls."

## ENTREPRENEURS

"First-time entrepreneurs have to do their research, and they should be very passionate about what they are doing. Passion is the No. 1 ingredient for success . . . because it's necessary in order to withstand the challenges and difficulties one will face.

"You have to completely believe in what you are doing, and a knowledge of business is useful, but I would mention that passion, momentum and focus are crucial. It's good to read books by successful people . . . A good one for entrepreneurs is the recent book I wrote with Robert Kiyosaki, *Midas Touch*."

### Source
"7 Smart Things Donald Trump Told Me," by Geoffrey James, Inc.com, May 1, 2012.

*www.inc.com/geoffrey-james/7-smart-things-to-learn-from-donald-trump.html*

# GOLF

"Golf is the sport of business . . . I've made deals on a golf course that I would have never, ever [have] made over a lunch. I actually told the people at Wharton, 'You should give a course in golf.' There's something about the camaraderie. You get to know people better, they're your partner. I've always said about Obama that I don't mind that he plays golf, but he should play golf with people he wants to make agreements with."

**Source**

"Donald Trump: Let golf be for the rich elite," by Daniel Roberts, Fortune.com, July 1, 2015.

*http://fortune.com/2015/07/01/donald-trump-golf-rich-elite/*

# KEEPING OPTIONS OPEN

*Regarding the then undeveloped land, the West Side yards.* "I continue to keep all my other options open too, because, as I've said, it's the only way you truly protect yourself. If the residential real estate market remains strong, I'll undoubtedly do very well selling large, river-view apartments in that location. If the market generally falls—and that can only be temporary in a city like New York—I may choose to build only the shopping complex. I'll do very, very well just with that."

**Source**

*Trump: The Art of the Deal* (Random House, 1987).

## In Context

A prime example of how Trump works the art of a deal, the eventual development of what he termed "A West Side Story" shows the power of persistence and keeping all the options open.

As he wrote in the opening lines of Chapter 13 of *The Art of the Deal*, "The toughest business decision I ever made was giving up my option on the West Side yards—seventy-eight riverfront acres between 59th Street and 72nd Street—in the summer of 1979. The easiest business decision I ever made was buying back those same hundred yards in January 1985."

His persistence eventually paid off. As he wrote, "It has been reported that I paid $95 million for the West Side yards, or about $1 million an acre, which is not far from the correct figure."

In June 2005, as Charles V. Bagli reported in the *New York Times* ("Trump Group Selling West Side Parcel for $1.8 Billion," June 1, 2005), "A consortium of Hong Kong investors and Donald J. Trump are selling a stretch of riverfront land and three buildings on the Upper West Side for about $1.8 billion in the largest residential sale in city history and in the latest example of a rocketing housing market." It was, the paper notes, the "onetime railroad yard . . . which has been turned into a luxury enclave known variously as Riverside South and Trump Place . . ."

## LOSING GROUND

"Look, I'm an artist. Right now when you look, you see the North Sea, the waves crashing against the shore, you see the magnificence of this body of water. I don't want to be looking at rusty windmills all over the place. Because that's what happens to them—they all turn to rust, and they're disgusting. And I said until such time as that project is killed, I'm not building anymore.

I'm not gonna be staring at windmills. And in my opinion, the wind farm will never happen. I think they'll back down. And when that happens, when they announce that they're gonna abandon it, then I'll start the second course."

## Source

"Donald Trump: I'm Huge!," by John Barton, GolfDigest.com, November 2014.

*www.golfdigest.com/magazine/2014-11/donald-trump-interview*

## In Context

As the *Guardian* (February 11, 2014) reported, "Donald Trump has bought a five-star golf resort on the west coast of Ireland after losing a legal action against a wind farm being built near his golf resort in Aberdeenshire. The billionaire property developer said that while he appealed against the court defeat in Scotland he would be diverting his energies to the exclusive Doonbeg golf and hotel complex on the Atlantic coastline of County Clare, restyling it the Trump International Golf Links, Ireland.

"Trump has taken the Scottish government to court over a decision to approve a major experimental wind farm in Aberdeen Bay, which will be about two miles south east of his planned golf resort . . . because it spoilt the view."

# NEGOTIATION

"Well, as I said, I study people and in every negotiation, I weigh how tough I should appear. I can be a killer and a nice guy. You have to be everything. You have to be strong. You have to be sweet. You have to be ruthless. And I don't think any of it can be learned. Either you have it or you don't. And that is why most kids can get straight A's in school but fail in life."

### Source

"Donald Trump," by Glenn Plaskin, *Playboy*, March 1990.

### In Context

Citing himself as a master negotiator, Trump feels our country's politicians and ambassadors and trade negotiators are insufficiently skilled in the art of negotiation. In *The Art of the Deal* he explains, "My style of deal-making is quite simple and straightforward. I aim very high, and then I just keep pushing and pushing and pushing to get what I'm after. Sometimes I settle for less than I sought, but in most cases I still end up with what I want."

# NET WORTH

"His debt is a very small percentage of value, and at very low interest rates. As of this date, Mr. Trump's net worth is in excess of TEN BILLION DOLLARS."

### Source

"Donald Trump's Team Says His 'Massive' Net Worth Is More Than 'TEN BILLION DOLLARS,'" by Igor Bobic, HuffPost Politics, HuffingtonPost .com, July 15, 2015.

*www.huffingtonpost.com/entry/donald-trump-net-worth_55a6a342e4b 0c5f0322c1726*

### In Context

Trump sued author Timothy L. O'Brien, who wrote that The Donald's net worth was far less than he claimed—Trump lost the lawsuit. A New Jersey appeals court decided: "There were no significant internal inconsistencies in the information provided by the confidential sources, nor was there 'reliable' information that contradicted their reports, so as to provide evidence of actual malice. Nothing suggests that O'Brien was subjectively aware of the falsity of his source's figures or that he had actual doubts as to the information's accuracy." Later, James Surowiecki wrote, in "Donald Trump's Sales Pitch" (*New Yorker*, August 10, 2015): "It's impossible to get a definitive accounting of his wealth, since almost all of it is in assets—mainly real estate—that don't have clear market values. Still, he's clearly enormously rich. Bloomberg estimates his wealth at $2.9 billion, while *Forbes* pegs it at $4.1 billion . . . But Trump will have none of that: thanks to the value of his brand, he says, he's worth at least a cool ten billion. This number seems so absurdly over the top as to be self-defeating."

As for Trump's own valuation, his one-page report, dated July 15, 2015, to the FEC stated a net worth of approximately $8.7 billion, but his people subsequently revised it, citing rising real estate value among his holdings, to more than $10 billion.

## OIL PRICES

"The biggest problem we have, no matter—and it's always going to be—every time I watch in the morning the various shows, right, the business shows. Every time the economy gets good, oil goes up. Gets good, again. Gets good, again. So what they do is they systematically destroy any momentum you get. Because oil should be selling at $25 to $30 a barrel right now. The economy stinks throughout the world, other than for China and for certain OPEC nations where they're making a bundle."

**Source**

"Transcript: My Interview with Donald Trump, Part 2," by George Stephanopoulos, ABC News, August 17, 2011.

*http://blogs.abcnews.com/george/2011/08/full-transcript-my-interview-with-donald-trump-part-2.html*

# PAYING TAXES

"I fight like hell to pay as little as possible for two reasons. Number one, I'm a businessman. And that's the way you're supposed to do it . . . The other reason is that I hate the way our government spends our taxes. I hate the way they waste our money. Trillions and trillions of dollars of waste and abuse. And I hate it."

**Source**

"Donald Trump Says He's 'Probably the First Candidate in the History of Politics' Willing to Admit This," by Jason Howerton, TheBlaze.com, August 3, 2015.

*www.theblaze.com/stories/2015/08/03/donald-trump-says-hes-probably-the-first-candidate-in-the-history-of-politics-to-admit-this-about-his-taxes/*

# PERSONAL BRAND

"A brand saves time for the public. They will know a gold standard brand because the name will stand for the gold standard. It takes the guesswork out. Chanel did this with her fashion and fragrances and was extremely successful.

"It has been done before, but the Trump brand is very comprehensive— it's not just beautiful buildings, but golf courses, books, a hit television show, a men's clothing line and fragrance, and a hotel collection. This list goes on. But every aspect of the Trump brand will signify the best because that is our standard.

"The first building I put my name on was Trump Tower, which has become a top tourist site and remains as beautiful as when it opened in 1983. That was the beginning, for me, of the Trump brand."

### Source

"7 Smart Things Donald Trump Told Me," by Geoffrey James, Inc.com, May 2, 2012.

*www.inc.com/geoffrey-james/7-smart-things-to-learn-from-donald-trump.html*

# PRESS COVERAGE

"Mark—You are a total loser—and your book (and your writings) suck! Best wishes, Donald. PS: And I hear it is selling badly."

### Source

"Donald Trump's handwritten war with the press," by Ben Terris, *Washington Post*, June 17, 2015.

*www.washingtonpost.com/news/style-blog/wp/2015/06/17/donald-trumps-handwritten-war-with-the-press/*

### In Context

Trump is frequently asked for interviews, which he views as a double-edged sword: Press coverage helps build his brand, but negative press coverage tarnishes it. Mark Singer's profile of Trump in *Character Studies* (Mariner Books, 2005), reprinted from the *New Yorker* ("Trump Solo," May

19, 1997), obviously rubbed him the wrong way. In the piece, Trump told Singer: "I think the thing I'm worst at is managing the press. The press portrays me as a wild flamethrower. In actuality, I think I'm much different from that. I think I'm totally inaccurately portrayed."

When Singer speculates as to whether or not Trump has a soul, he's skating on thin ice. It's no wonder, then, that in one of his books (*Trump: The Art of the Comeback*), Trump titles one of his chapters, "The Press and Other Germs."

## PRESSURE

"No. 1: I could handle pressure. A lot of my friends couldn't and just took the gas. I knew tough guys, or people who I thought were tough but who crawled into a corner, put their thumbs in their mouths and cried, 'Mummy, I want to go home.' I didn't lose sleep, I never, ever gave up, and I fought hard to survive. The biggest thing I learnt is that economic cycles don't last forever, they go up and they go down. And whatever you try to do to keep a cycle going, they end. Period. If you study the financial charts from 1900 to now, it's almost a perfect roller-coaster graph, it's amazing."

### Source

"Donald Trump on sex, money and politics," by Piers Morgan, *British GQ*, GQ-magazine.co.uk, August 7, 2015, reprinted from the print edition published December 2008.

*www.gq-magazine.co.uk/entertainment/articles/2011-05/17/ gq-entertainment-donald-trump-interview-piers-morgan*

## SELF-MADE RICH PEOPLE

"Rich people are great survivors and, by nature, they fall into two categories—those who have inherited and those who've made it. Those who have inherited and chosen not to do anything are generally very timid, afraid of losing what they've got, and who can blame them? Others are great risk takers and produce a hell of a lot more or go bust."

### Source

"Donald Trump," by Glenn Plaskin, *Playboy*, March 1990.

## SELF-PROMOTION

"Because if you don't, probably nobody else will. Whether I'm building the best buildings in Chicago, New York, California or wherever I happen to be building, I think I get credit for being a great promoter. Actually, what I am is a great builder. I build great things and become successful, and everybody talks about them. I like to be remembered as somebody with a high standard of taste who got the job done and also put lots of people to work, made lots of money for the poor and fed a lot of families."

### Source

"Donald Trump," by Glenn Plaskin, *Playboy*, March 1990.

# TIMING

"No matter how good you are, timing is so important; and some people have timing, and some people don't, and I have it."

### Source

"Trump grows up," by Ben Schreckinger, Politico.com, July 15, 2015. *www.politico.com/story/2015/07/donald-trump-grows-up-politico-interview-120196*

# TRACK RECORD

"I'm a great believer in two things: people and track records. There's an old expression on Wall Street: 'It seems that it's always the same people who get lucky.' The fact is, these people are 'lucky' for various reasons. They do their research, have tremendous instincts and brainpower, and then there's the X-factor—that special ingredient that enables people to make money."

### Source

*Trump: The Art of the Comeback*, "Investing: Caveat Emptor" (Times Books, 1997).

### In Context

The difference between what you say you're going to do and what you've done is your track record. It's the critical difference between opinion and fact. At the first Republican presidential debate (August 6, 2015), Chris Wallace asked: "Mr. Trump, you talk a lot about how you are the person on this stage to grow the economy. I want to ask you about your business record. Trump corporations, casinos, and hotels have declared bankruptcy four times over the last quarter-century.

"In 2011, you told *Forbes* magazine: 'I've used the laws of this country to my advantage.' But as the same time, financial experts involved in those bankruptcies say that lenders to your companies lost billions of dollars.

"Question, sir, with that record: why should we trust you to run the nation's business?"

Trump responded, citing his track record: "Out of hundreds of deals that I've done, on four occasions I've taken advantage of the [bankruptcy] laws of this country, like other people . . . Four times, I've taken advantage of the laws. And frankly, so has everybody else in my position. The fact is, I built a net worth of more than $10 billion. I have a great, great company. I employ thousands of people. And I'm very proud of the job I did . . . Let me tell you about the lenders. First of all, these lenders aren't babies. These are total killers. They are not the nice, sweet little people that you think, okay?" In other words, over the course of a long business career, Trump has succeeded far more often than he has failed. It's risky business, and everyone knows what they're getting into—taking calculated risks to potentially make, or lose, a fortune.

Nobody wins all the time, but only losers lose all the time. It's there in black and white, in the track record. The numbers always speak loudly for themselves.

## THE WORKING CLASS

"I love real estate, I love buildings. I'm building the tallest residential tower in the world right opposite the United Nations now. I love it. I love going there. I love being with the workers. I love walking in the concrete. I mean, it's hard to believe. And those are the people who vote for me actually, the people building those buildings, all of those buildings all over the country. The workers are the ones that really like me.

"I've often said: The rich people hate me and the workers love me. Now, the rich people that know me like me, but the rich people that don't know me, they truly dislike me."

## Source

"Transcript: Donald Trump announces plans to form presidential exploratory committee," *Larry King Live*, CNN.com, October 8, 1999.

*www.cnn.com/ALLPOLITICS/stories/1999/10/08/trump.transcript/*

# Trump on Trump

## APOLOGIZING

"I think apologizing is a great thing, but you have to be wrong . . . I will absolutely apologize, sometime in the hopefully distant future, if I'm ever wrong."

### Source

"Donald Trump on *Tonight Show*: The Good, The Bad, and The Delusional," by Jessica Roy, TVGuide.com, September 12, 2015.

*www.tvguide.com/news/donald-trump-tonight-show*

## ASSERTIVENESS

"Even in elementary school, I was a very assertive, aggressive kid. In the second grade I actually gave a teacher a black eye—I punched my music teacher because I didn't think he knew anything about music and I almost got expelled. I'm not proud of that, but it's clear evidence that even early on I had a tendency to stand up and make my opinions known in a very forceful way. The difference now is that I like to use my brain instead of my fists."

## Source

*Trump: The Art of the Deal,* "Growing Up" (Random House, 1987).

## In Context

What was once a liability turned into an asset, when Trump uses it to fuel his negotiations. Even his critics admit that, when it comes to negotiation, Trump is tough and drives a hard bargain. In *Trump: Surviving at the Top,* he writes: "I respect smart, tough people the way others admire great athletes or entertainers—even when these people are unpopular or down on their luck."

## BEING RECOGNIZED

"You want to know what total recognition is? I'll tell you how you know you've got it. When the Nigerians on the street corners who don't speak a word of English, who have no clue, who're selling watches for some guy in New Jersey—when you walk by and those guys say, 'Trump! Trump!' That's total recognition."

## Source

"Trump Solo," by Mark Singer, *New Yorker,* May 19, 1997.
*www.newyorker.com/magazine/1997/05/19/trump-solo*

## In Context

Given that New York City is Trump's stomping grounds, it's not surprising that the man on the street recognizes him on sight. But it's TV that often brings a prominent and successful figure to the masses in a way that print media alone cannot. Case in point: *The Apprentice* television show, which gave him his signature line—"You're fired!"—made him a household name.

Predictably, when NBC recently ousted Trump from the network, the act prompted gleeful headlines, many with variations of "You're Fired!"

Robert Siegel ("NBC Dumps Donald Trump Over Comments On Mexican Immigrants," NPR.org, June 29, 2015), explained: "NBC is done with Donald Trump. The network has severed its ties with the billionaire following controversial remarks about Mexicans. He made those when he announced that he's running for president. NPR TV critic Eric Deggans says NBC's move threatens a Trump-centered media empire, which includes two beauty pageants and a reality TV show."

Trump's version ("The Donald Conversation: Murdoch, Ailes, NBC and the Rush of Being TV's 'Ratings Machine,'" by Janice Min, HollywoodReporter.com, August 19, 2015) of what happened: "The primary tension I had was that they wanted to do *The Apprentice*, and they were very angry that I didn't do it . . . I read a story two weeks ago from somebody that didn't understand, where they said NBC cut ties with Trump. They didn't cut ties with me, I cut ties with them out of respect. But they were very upset."

## DISASTERS

"Well, I've responded very much to disasters. I've had, you know, fires in buildings, big buildings. I've had economic changes where the world crashed in the early nineties, and I came out stronger than I was before. And I didn't go bankrupt like many people that were forced into bankruptcy, and they were forced into, like, you know disasters never to be heard from again. I came out stronger than I was before. There was an old expression in the early nineties—survive til '95 that I made up, and I gave. And I actually became much stronger. But I've gone through, I've watched economic problems happen. Eight years ago, nine years ago when I was buying and everybody else was selling because they had no money and I did have a lot of money and I bought a lot of great assets. And you know, I've gone through a lot of different things, and I've come out on top always."

## Source

"Donald Trump On the Day He Took the Pledge," by Hugh Hewitt, transcript, HughHewitt.com, September 3, 2015.

*www.hughhewitt.com/donald-trump-on-the-day-he-took-the-pledge/*

# DISTRUST

"I saw people really taking *advantage* of Fred and the lesson I learned was *always to keep up my guard 100 percent*, whereas he didn't. He didn't feel that there was really reason for that, which is a *fatal* mistake in life. People are too trusting. I'm a very *untrusting* guy. I study people all the time, automatically; it's my way of life, for better or worse."

## Source

"Donald Trump," by Glenn Plaskin, *Playboy*, March 1990.

## In Context

The firstborn son, Fred Trump Jr., was expected to follow in his father's footsteps but found business was not his passion. He became an airline pilot and "died from heart failure brought on by acute alcoholism," according to *Playboy*. Donald Trump, who does not consume alcohol or coffee, credits his older brother, who cautioned him against smoking and drinking—two habits Donald has reinforced with his own children. On *The Brody File* ("The Human Side: Donald Trump Talks about the Death of His Brother to

Alcoholism," by David Brody, CBN News, airdate April 2011, *http://blogs.cbn .com/thebrodyfile/archive/2015/07/12/the-human-side-donald-trump-talks-about-the-death-of.aspx*), Donald Trump said that he was so insistent, and repetitive, in warning his children about those twin evils that it got "to a point where my daughter Ivanka would say, 'Don't say it anymore, don't say it anymore.' But literally once a week, I would say no, and I think they got through that horrible stage of big drinking and drugs and even smoking. So they don't smoke, they don't take drugs, and they don't drink. I think, I hope."

## ENTERTAINER, POLITICIAN, OR BOTH?

"As far as temperament—and we all know that—as far as temperament, I think I have a great temperament. I built a phenomenal business with incredible, iconic assets, one of the really truly great real-estate businesses.

"And I may be an entertainer, because I've had tremendous success with number-one bestsellers all over the place, with *The Apprentice* and everything else I've done.

"But I will tell you this: What I am far and away greater than an entertainer is a businessman, and that's the kind of mindset this country needs to bring it back, because we owe $19 trillion right now, $19 trillion, and you need this kind of thinking to bring our country back.

"And believe me, my temperament is very good, very calm. But we will be respected outside of this country. We are not respected now."

### Source
"Transcript: Read the Full Text of the Second Republican Debate," by Ryan Teague Beckwith, Time.com, September 16, 2015.

*http://time.com/4037239/second-republican-debate-transcript-cnn/*

## In Context

During the second Republican debate, Carly Fiorina said, "You know, I think Mr. Trump is a wonderful entertainer. He's been terrific at that business."

Trump is undeniably an entertainer, but as he's repeatedly pointed out in numerous interviews, he's had a long career as a successful businessman. Debate moderator Jake Tapper compared the two as business people: "Ms. Fiorina, you were CEO of Hewlett-Packard. Donald Trump says you, quote, 'ran HP into the ground,' you laid off tens of thousands of people, you got viciously fired. For voters looking to someone with private-sector experience to create American jobs, why should they pick you and not Donald Trump?"

Trump, during the debate, added: "The head of the Yale business school, Jeffrey Sonnenfeld, wrote a paper recently, one of the worst tenures for a CEO that he has ever seen, ranked one of the top twenty in the history of business. The company is a disaster and continues to be a disaster . . . When Carly says the revenues went up, that's because she bought Compaq. It was a terrible deal, and it really led to the destruction of the company. Now, one other company before that was Lucent. Carly was at Lucent before that. And Lucent turned out to be a catastrophe also. So I only say this: She can't run any of my companies. That I can tell you."

# FRAGILITY OF LIFE

"Life is fragile. It doesn't matter who you are, how good you are at what you do, how many beautiful buildings you put up, or how many people know your name. No one on earth can be totally secure, because nothing can completely protect you from life's tragedies and the relentless passage of time."

## Source

*Trump: Surviving at the Top,* "Now for the Hard Part," (Random House, 1990).

### In Context

On October 10, 1989, "a day that changed my life," Trump got the news that three of his chief executives had died in a helicopter crash. He got it in the worst possible way, from a reporter for CBS-TV news who phoned him: "Five dead, Mr. Trump. All in body bags. Any comment?"

The leased helicopter had a catastrophic mechanical failure, killing all five on board. Trump said it made him realize that nothing can protect oneself from the randomness of the universe, that security in this world is an illusion.

Trump, now sixty-nine years old and in his third marriage, has come to appreciate that life itself is fragile and precious. The people near and dear to him—his family, friends, and employees—are what ultimately matters. Unlike possessions like fancy cars, estate homes, helicopters, and commercial buildings, human lives are irreplaceable.

## HANDSHAKING

*When approached by a man in 21 Club in Manhattan, who just emerged from the restroom:* "Now, I have two choices. Don't shake it, and here's a man that for the rest of his life will hate Donald Trump. But I don't want that. I have a heart. Or shake it. And you don't know what you are shaking. And you know what I did? I shook his hand. And then, I didn't eat as well, because I didn't know where his hand was. But I can tell you it wasn't in a very good place."

### Source

"After Roasting, Trump Reacts in Character," by Michael Barbaro, *New York Times*, May 1, 2011; print version May 2, 2011.

*www.nytimes.com/2011/05/02/nyregion/after-roasting-trump-reacts-in-character.html?_r=0*

## In Context

Call it a personal idiosyncrasy, but Trump has never been a fan of shaking hands. He considers it unsanitary.

As he wrote in *Trump: How to Get Rich*, "It is a terrible practice. So often, I see someone who is obviously sick, with a bad cold or the flu, who approaches me and says, 'Mr. Trump, I would like to shake your hand.' It's a medical fact that this is how germs are spread. I wish we could follow the Japanese custom of bowing instead."

## LEARNING FROM LIFE

"Well, a lot of people ask me a question, 'If you had it to do again, what would you do?' And I always give the same answer. I consider life—because it's—it's a question that you can't do anything about. And I'm a realist. The main thing I want to do, everybody makes mistakes, we all mistakes, you've had 'em, I've had 'em, we've all had 'em. The key is you have to learn from your mistakes. So, it doesn't happen again. So, I don't want to do anything over. I've had a great life. I've had an amazing life. I've really enjoyed my life. I have great kids, great family. But I really just say one thing about all of that; there's no make-up, but you have to learn from whatever it is."

### Source

"Donald Trump Interview: Transcript Part Two," by George Stephanopoulos, ABC News, April 19, 2011.

*http://blogs.abcnews.com/george/2011/04/donald-trump-interview-transcript-part-two.html*

# MISTAKES

"You have to learn from your successes and your failures. And if you don't learn from mistakes, then you're a fool. Now, ideally you want to watch other people and learn from their mistakes, because that's less costly and less traumatic. But . . . I wouldn't want to do it much differently. For instance, I was told, 'Don't do *The Apprentice* because it can never succeed on television, because very few shows do succeed.' And I did it against the wishes of many people . . . So you have to just sort of go by your wits."

### Source
"Donald Trump," by Candace Taylor, TheRealDeal.com, 2009.
*http://therealdeal.com/closings/donald-trump/*

# NAYSAYERS

"If you want to be a success, you have to get used to frequently hearing the word *no* and ignoring it . . . Quitters do not get anywhere. You will not be successful if you listen to nos . . . People are not looking out for you. They do not want the best for you; they are looking out for themselves. When most people say no, they are doing it to further their own ends. Do not let somebody's arbitrary no stop you."

### Source
*Think Big and Kick Ass in Business and Life*, with Bill Zanker, "Do You Have What It Takes?" (HarperCollins, 2007).

## In Context

On the face of it, Donald Trump doesn't need the headaches that come with a run for political office—especially the presidency. But from the very beginning, naysayers have predicted his imminent downfall. As Errol Louis of the *New York Daily News* ("Donald Trump is not a clown: Signs say he actually wants to win—and his books reveal real policy ideas," August 4, 2015) points out: "I can't count how many friends and strangers have stopped me on the street with a variation on the question: When is Donald Trump going to drop out of the race for president? I inevitably answer that I don't have the slightest idea—and neither does anybody else—but we should assume that, like any candidate, he'll try to remain in the race until the outcome becomes obvious. When that might happen is anybody's guess, although a fair number of pundits and journalists have already concluded, prematurely in my view, that the end of Trump's political career is right around the corner."

At the first Republican presidential debate, even one of Trump's fellow debaters had to give him his due. Ohio governor John Kasich said, "We need to take lessons from Donald Trump if we're really going to learn it. Here is the thing about Donald Trump. Donald Trump is hitting a nerve in this country. He is. He's hitting a nerve. People are frustrated. They're fed up. They don't think the government is working for them. And for people who want to just tune him out, they're making a mistake."

Among those underestimating him: on the first Republican presidential debate, the editorial board of the *Washington Post* ("Only a handful of GOP candidates are living in the real world," August 7, 2015) concluded: "There were many other candidates who couldn't muster the courage, were frighteningly out-of-touch, or both, with Mr. Trump far and away the lead offender. These Republicans offer a one-way ticket to political and policy disaster. Mr. Trump is not a credible candidate."

There are others who thought Trump would have quit by now, but as Errol Louis observed, Trump shows no signs of quitting: "We should assume that, like any candidate, he'll try to remain in the race until the outcome becomes obvious."

If Trump listened to his critics, he would never have run; having run, they've said he wouldn't file financial disclosure forms, which he did; they've called him names ("a feckless blowhard," wrote the *Des Moines Register*), and he hasn't quit. When he stood center stage at the first Republican presidential debate, he took immediate fire from the moderators, who singled him out with a question to which they already knew the answer: Would he pledge his support to the Republican front-runner if he was not the party nominee? And would he run as an independent?

Many people have said *no*, to which Trump has, in effect, replied: I don't care what you think.

Bottom line: Trump is in the game to win. Initially ridiculed by the media for having the audacity to announce his candidacy, he's now being taken more seriously by the GOP and some in the media. Noted Susan Page of *USA Today* ("Reveling in quick rise, Trump already mulls running mate," October 23, 2015), "It is increasingly hard to deny that the 69-year-old celebrity billionaire is also a credible Republican presidential nominee."

## PERSISTENCE

"Very often I meet people with great ideas but they lack the tenacity required to make it, and sometimes they lack the skills. You have to know everything you can about what you're doing. Not everything works every time. So you have to just keep at it and never give up. I've seen people who give up too soon. There are risks involved, of course, so the person also has to have the ability to live with that risk. Some people don't have that in their personality, and some people fail to develop it."

### Source

"The Monday Interview with Donald Trump and Robert Kiyosaki," by Dick Donahue, PublishersWeekly.com, October 3, 2011.

*www.publishersweekly.com/pw/by-topic/authors/interviews/article/48931-the-monday-interview-with-donald-trump-and-robert-kiyosaki.html*

### In Context

On Twitter on May 21, 2014, Trump wrote: "Persistence is a key for success. Don't give up. Continue to Think Big and you will be able to close deals." In *Trump: Never Give Up*, he talks about the difficulties he encountered when constructing Trump Tower. "Nothing was easy from day one," he writes. "To begin the saga, it took me almost three years to even get a response from the man who controlled the land I wanted to buy. I made calls and wrote letter after letter. I learned a lot about persistence, but I also learned that if you are passionate about something, receiving zero encouragement still won't discourage you. I just plain wouldn't give up."

Though Trump is a magnet for criticism, even the most vocal among them have to admit that Trump has a pit bullish penchant for persisting, no matter how many obstacles are thrown up, and no matter how long it takes.

# PREDATORS

"Look, we are worse than the lions in the jungle. Worse than any predator. Lions hunt for food, to live. We hunt for sport. Our hunting involves doing lots of bad things to other people, whether it's stealing their money or whatever.

People are bad, they really are! They're evil in many cases! So you have to keep your left up [a boxing term]. People have to respect you, if they don't respect you then, even if they are fairly honest, they will start to steal from you. That's the way it is. Pretty sad, but true."

## Source

"Donald Trump on sex, money and politics," by Piers Morgan, *British GQ*, GQ-magazine.co.uk, August 7, 2015, reprinted from the print edition published December 2008.

*www.gq-magazine.co.uk/entertainment/articles/2011-05/17/ gq-entertainment-donald-trump-interview-piers-morgan*

## In Context

On a geopolitical level, one of Trump's most vocal criticisms is that the United States is like the late comedian Rodney Dangerfield: "I don't get no respect!" Trump argues that we give foreign nations not merely millions but *billions* of dollars, and often get little, or nothing, in return.

Case in point: As Trump writes in *Time to Get Tough*: "Pakistan is not our friend. We've given them billions and billions of dollars, and what did we get? Betrayal and disrespect—and much worse. When one of our helicopters was downed during the Osama bin Laden raid, Pakistan handed it over to China so the Chinese engineers could study it and steal the technology we spent billions of dollars developing. The Pakistanis think we're a bunch of dopes."

In the same chapter, "Strengthen American Muscle," he points out that when we found Osama bin Laden, he was "in Pakistan right next door to one of Pakistan's most prestigious military academies. What does that tell you? It tells me that Pakistan knew where Osama was all along."

# PRENUPTIAL AGREEMENT

"For example, due to the vastness and complexity of my business, it would have taken ten or fifteen years in many different courts, states, and perhaps even countries to finalize my situation with either [of my former wives] Ivana or Marla. My financial life would have been officially over, and certainly I wouldn't be able to write a book. Many millions would have been paid to lawyers. It would have been ridiculous. In terms of wheeling and dealing, which is essentially my life, I would've been reduced to court orders and litigation. My business would have been in total disarray."

## Source

*Trump: The Art of the Comeback*, "The Art of the Prenup: The Engagement Wring" (Times Books, 1997).

## In Context

Donald Trump's first two marriages both ended in divorce. "I blame myself because my business was so powerful for me," Trump told CNN *State of the Union* host Jake Tapper. ("Donald Trump Pressed On How 'Traditional' His 3 Marriages Are," by Elise Foley, HuffPost Politics, June 28, 2015.)

As Trump points out, both of his former wives fought their prenups and lost. He has, of course, a prenup with his third wife, the former Melania Knauss, who on January 22, 2005, gave him his fifth child, Barron William Trump. *New York Magazine* ("With This Ring (and This Contract), I Thee Wed," by Geoffrey Gray, March 27, 2006) quoted Trump: "It's a hard, painful, ugly tool. Believe me, there's nothing fun about it. But there comes a time when you have to say, 'Darling, I think you're magnificent, and I care for you deeply, but if things don't work out, this is what you're going to get.'"

Trump disagrees with the idea that, in marriage, all you need is love. What you *need* is a rock solid prenup. Ask Paul McCartney.

## RUNNING AMOK

*Glenn Plaskin,* Playboy *magazine:* "In the book *Trumped!*, an unauthorized biography, your former employee John O'Donnell describes your ripping upholstery out of a limo, ramming your fist through tile in a casino, yelling at pilots for rough landings."

*Trump:* "O'Donnell is a loser. He totally made that up. I hardly even knew this guy. He wasn't very good at what he did. I've had many books written about me, and in almost all instances they just make things up and say whatever they want, even if it's total nonsense. I ripped the interior out of limousines? Give me a break."

### Source
"Donald Trump," by Glenn Plaskin, *Playboy*, March 1990.

### In Context
John R. O'Donnell, a former president and CEO of Trump Plaza Hotel & Casino, wrote a tell-all book that was very highly critical of Trump and his first wife, Ivana. O'Donnell's book depicted his boss as a demanding, impossibly difficult man whose anger and profanity-laced language was delivered at high volume. There is no real evidence that confirms or disproves O'Donnell's assertions.

O'Donnell's book illustrates why Trump is always on his guard and highly critical of books written about him, authorized or not.

# THIN-SKINNED

"I was listening to you talk about Bush and Rubio and a couple of others, and you sort of forgot to mention my name even though I'm creaming them all in the polls."

## Source

"'My god, stop being so thin-skinned!' Joe Scarborough just had an incredible Donald Trump interview," by Colin Campbell, BusinessInsider .com, July 24, 2015.

*www.businessinsider.com/joe-scarborough-donald-trump-thin-skinned-2015-7*

## In Context

Joe Scarborough is an MSNBC anchor who is on friendly terms with Trump. In the interview Campbell cited, when Trump told Scarborough of his omission, the latter responded: "Donald, what are you talking about? What are you talking about! We've been talking about you for a week! What are you talking about, Donald? How thin is your skin? I've been talking about you for a week!"

Campbell noted that the back and forth prompted Scarborough to demand, "Donald, you aren't really that thin-skinned, are you? We have been talking about you so much. This is hilarious. You are incredibly thin-skinned, my friend."

Trump agreed. "Yes, oh, I'm thin-skinned," he told Scarborough.

In the past, Bill Maher, the *Huffington Post*, writers for *New Republic*, and others have pointed out that, in their opinion, Donald Trump has a thin skin, so Scarborough is not alone in thinking so.

# Timeline

*This abbreviated timeline is a brief overview that gives a sense of Donald J. Trump's personal and business milestones. By intent I have provided some but not all information on the Trump Organization's holdings, which is beyond the scope of this book, because they encompass real estate around the world, hotels, golf courses, entertainment and television ventures, publications, or branded merchandise. The interested reader can find those details at www.trump.com.*

Note: DT = Donald Trump.

## 1946

Donald John Trump is born on June 14 in Queens, New York, to Frederick C. Trump, a real estate developer, and Mary MacLeod.

His other siblings include: Maryanne Trump Barry (federal appeals court judge, District of New Jersey), Fred Trump Jr. (airline pilot; deceased, 1981), Robert Trump (executive vice president, the Trump Organization), and Elizabeth Trump Grau (an administrative assistant in the banking industry).

## 1950–1959

DT attends the coed Kew-Forest School, a pre-K–12 college preparatory school in Forest Hills, New York. He was, by his own admission, a fractious child. "Even in elementary school, I was a very assertive, aggressive kid." (*Trump: The Art of the Deal*.) According to the *Washington Post* (July 17, 2015), Trump's father "was on the governing board. Behavior problems led to Donald's exit from the school, at which point he was sent to the New York Military Academy at age thirteen by his parents, who, according to Biography.com, hoped 'the discipline of the school would channel his energy in a positive manner.'"

## 1959–1964

DT enrolls in the New York Military Academy because "my father decided to send me to a military school, assuming that a little military training might be good for me. I wasn't thrilled about the idea, but it turned out he was right. I stayed through my senior year, and along the way I learned a lot about discipline, and about channeling my aggression into achievement. In my senior year I was appointed a captain of the cadets." (*Trump: The Art of the Deal*.)

June 1964 DT graduates from the New York Military Academy, having shone academically as an athlete and a student leader.

## 1964–1966

DT attends Fordham University then transfers to the Wharton School of Finance at the University of Pennsylvania. While in school, DT joins the family business, Trump Management Co., which focuses on the boroughs surrounding Manhattan.

## 1968

DT graduates with a BA in economics from the University of Pennsylvania's Wharton School of Finance. "At the time," he wrote in *Trump: The Art of the Deal*, "if you were going to make a career in business, Wharton was the place to go. Harvard Business School may produce a lot of CEOs—guys who manage public companies—but the real entrepreneurs all seemed to go to Wharton . . . Perhaps the most important thing I learned at Wharton was not to be overly impressed by academic credentials . . . In my opinion, that degree doesn't prove very much, but a lot of people I do business with take it very seriously, and it's considered very prestigious."

(Three of Trump's children, Donald Jr., Eric, and Ivanka, have joined the family business. *Business Insider*, citing Jack Dickey [Time.com, August 16, 2015], notes that the Trump Organization has "a reported 22,000 employees, with nine luxury hotels, 17 golf courses and 18 luxury residential properties worldwide . . . Don Jr. manages the existing property portfolio, Ivanka oversees the family hotels, and Eric manages the family's golf assets.")

## 1971

DT moves into a studio apartment in Manhattan, at 75th Street and Third Avenue. "Moving into that apartment was probably more exciting for me than moving, fifteen years later, into the top three floors of Trump Tower. I was a kid from Queens who worked in Brooklyn, and suddenly I had an apartment on the Upper East Side." (*Trump: The Art of the Deal.*) He begins his career as a real estate developer.

## 1972

DT scores his first major deal: the sale of Swifton Village in Cincinnati, Ohio, for $6.75 million.

## 1974

DT buys property on the Hudson River, known as the West Side Yards. On its ninety-two acres, Trump builds a complex called Television City, eventually renamed Trump City. According to Observer.com (Eliot Brown, August 5, 2008), "Mr. Trump sold off much of his stake in the mid-1990s to a group of investors from Hong Kong . . . In mid-2005, Extell and the Carlyle Group bought the remaining property for $1.76 billion, though Mr. Trump later filed a lawsuit claiming his Hong Kong investors could have gotten a higher price."

DT becomes president of the family business, Trump Management Co., and later, in 1980, renames it the Trump Organization.

## 1976

DT and Hyatt Corporation partner to buy the Commodore Hotel, transforming it into the Grand Hyatt. On October 7, 1996, Hyatt buys out Trump's share for $142 million.

## 1977

DT marries Ivana Marie Zelnícková, a New York fashion model. On December 31 the Trumps have their first of three children: Donald Trump Jr.

## 1979

After buying "air rights" from Tiffany next door, DT buys the eleven-story department store Bonwit Teller on Fifth Avenue between 56th Street and 57th Street. He rebuilds it as a mixed-use building sixty-eight stories high housing retail shops, office buildings, and residential condominiums; the top three comprise his personal residence encompassing 30,000 square feet. The flagship building is named Trump Tower, which houses the Trump Organization.

## 1980

DT takes over the project to construct the Wollman ice skating rink in Central Park, after New York City tried and failed to develop it after spending $12 million and six years in the process. (The Trump Skating Rink, operated by the Trump Organization, is open for ice skating from October to April.)

DT opens the Grand Hyatt New York after extensive renovations.

## 1981

Ivanka Trump, the Trumps' second child, is born October 30. She later forms, with her brothers, Trump Hotel Collection. She starts her own name brand of clothing and accessories carried by high-end department stores. She currently works as an executive vice president of acquisitions and development for the family business and is the author of *The Trump Card: Playing to Win in Work and Life* (Touchstone, 2009).

## 1982

DT buys Harrah's, and renames it Trump Plaza.

## 1983

Trump Tower opens in midtown Manhattan and becomes a major tourist attraction.

DT becomes the owner of a football team, the New Jersey Generals, members of the United States Football League. The League folds after only three seasons.

## 1984

Eric Trump, the Trumps' third child, is born. Like his older brother and sister, he is destined to go into the family business; he is currently executive of acquisitions and development, specializing in construction. He owns Trump Winery, a 1,300-acre estate near Charlottesville, Virginia, that opened in 2011.

# 1985

DT buys Mar-a-Lago, a luxurious estate in Palm Beach, Florida. (The estate is now a private club called Mar-a-Lago Club.)

DT buys a rent-controlled apartment building at 106 Central Park South and the adjacent Barbizon Plaza Hotel, which he renovates and renames Trump Parc. Built in 1930, the building houses apartments for sale.

# 1987

DT publishes his first bestselling book, *Trump: The Art of the Deal*, from Random House.

# 1988

DT buys the Plaza Hotel at 59th Street and Fifth Avenue: $210 million for the real estate and $180 million for the hotel and its contents, totaling $390 million.

Trump sells the hotel in 1995 for $325 million; it is subsequently resold in 2004 for $675 million.

# 1989

DT buys the Eastern Air Lines shuttle for $365 million to form the Trump Shuttle, which flies between New York City and Boston on the hour. He sells it in 1992 to US Airways, which ended operations on October 17, 2015, and is now part of American Airlines.

The pilot, copilot, and three of DT's top executives, all involved in his casino operations, die in a helicopter crash when returning to Atlantic City.

DT begins construction on the Trump Taj Mahal, a major casino, at 1000 Boardwalk in Atlantic City, New Jersey.

## 1990

The real estate market crashes, dramatically affecting the Trump Organization. With determination and true grit, Trump manages to come back.

DT opens his third casino in Atlantic City, the Trump Taj Mahal; Michael Jackson performs for its opening ceremony. DT terms it the "eighth wonder of the world."

Trump sells the *Trump Princess*, his yacht, for $110 million, having bought it in 1987 for $30 million from the Sultan of Brunei.

## 1992

DT and Ivana Trump finalize their contentious and well-publicized public divorce, ending a fifteen-year marriage. Trump's business interests are protected by the terms of their prenuptial agreement. (Ivana later goes on to develop her own line of clothes, jewelry, and fashion products, selling on TV on cable shopping channels, and penning several books.)

## 1993

DT marries his second wife, Marla Maples, who gives birth to Tiffany Ariana Trump, born on October 13. (*People* magazine, on August 7, 2015, explained that Tiffany is a college student at the University of Pennsylvania, her father's alma mater. She has kept a low profile, but appeared at the first Republican debate in a show of family solidarity.)

## 1994

DT co-owns a NYC landmark, the Empire State Building. (The Associated Press, July 8, 2004, explains, "The arrangement did not cost Trump a dime, the developer said. In return for arranging equity financing for NS America, the group that bought the building for $45 million in October, Trump took over 50 percent ownership of the building.")

DT and his Japanese partner sell the Empire State Building to its long-term leaseholder for $57.5 million.

## 1996

DT assumes ownership of the Miss Universe Organization, known for its beauty pageants: Miss Universe, Miss USA, and Miss Teen USA. He pays $10 million for the properties.

## 1999

Donald divorces Marla Maples.

Maples, in the *New York Times*, November 14, 2012, told journalist Judith Newman, "With Donald, you know, I saw a real positive light in him. I could see the goodness, and we had this connection. It just happened that he had money. And money and power truly got in the way of the love that we had, to be very honest. If anything, it destroyed it."

Donald's view is quite different. As he explained in *Trump: The Art of the Comeback* (1997), "The fact is that time moves on and people change. You can be deeply in love when you get married, but a number of years later you just don't care to spend your life with that person anymore."

Donald's father, Fred Trump, dies.

DT forms an exploratory committee preparatory to a possible run for the presidential race for 2000 (October 7). Realizing that he'd never win as an independent, he switches allegiance to the Republican Party.

DT starts up Trump Model Management, showcasing supermodels.

DT, a registered Republican, switches allegiance to New York's Independence Party (the state's version of the Reform Party). He considered launching a presidential bid but felt a Reform Party candidate couldn't win, and chose not to run. "I understand this stuff. I understand good times and I understand bad times. I mean, why is a politician going to do a better job than I am?" (CNN.com/ALLPOLITICS, October 25, 1999.)

## 2001

DT registers as a Republican. (According to TheSmokingGun.com, August 6, 2015, Trump's history of voter registration has changed over the years:

July 1979, Republican; October 1999, Independence Party; August 2001, Democrat; December 2011, "I do not wish to enroll in a party"; and in April 2012, Republican.)

DT completes a condo development, Trump World Tower (845 United Nations Plaza), at a cost of $325 million.

## 2004

DT partners with NBC as the host and executive producer of *The Apprentice*. He later coproduces, with Mark Burnett, *The Celebrity Apprentice*. (The two shows have lasted fourteen seasons.)

DT speculates once again about running for the presidency, this time on the Republican Party ticket, but eventually decides not to.

*The Apprentice* is nominated for a Primetime Emmy Award but doesn't win. (Nominated again in 2005, 2006, and 2009, it doesn't win.)

## 2005

DT marries his third wife, Melania Knauss, at the Episcopal Church of Bethesda-by-the-Sea in Palm Beach, Florida, followed by a reception at his Mar-a-Lago Club. The wedding cost an estimated $1 million (January 22).

DT launches Trump University (name changed to Trump Entrepreneur Initiative in 2010). A CNN story (Jeanne Sahadi and Karen McGowan, July 24, 2015) reports that it promised "to teach students the mogul's investing techniques to get rich on real estate." DT is currently fighting two lawsuits from former students and from the New York attorney general. One of the suits, from a student who spent $36,000, said that "Trump University failed to deliver on its promises to provide a premier education."

DT, with a consortium of Hong Kong investors, sells "a stretch of river-front land and three buildings on the Upper West Side for about $1.8 billion in the largest residential sale in city history and in the latest example of a rocketing housing market." ("Trump Group Selling West Side . . . ," by Charles V. Bagli, *New York Times*, June 1, 2005.)

## 2006

DT locks horns with Rosie O'Donnell, then a co-host of *The View*, who asserted that Trump was "not a self-made man" but, instead, a "snake-oil salesman on *Little House on the Prairie*," and then takes digs at his marital history. Trump, who fights fire with ire, fires back, telling *People* magazine, "You can't make false statements. Rosie will rue the words she said [that he had declared personal bankruptcy, when in fact they were corporate bankruptcies]. I'll most likely sue her for making those false statements—and it'll be fun. Rosie's a loser. A real loser. I look forward to taking lots of money from my nice fat little Rosie."

Melania Knauss gives birth to DT's fifth child, Barron William Trump, on March 20.

DT buys property in Scotland, with an eye toward developing it as a golf resort. The course, costing $150 million to plan and build, opens seven years later near Aberdeen.

## 2007

DT gets a star on the Hollywood Walk of Fame for *The Apprentice*.

## 2009

DT files for his fourth corporate bankruptcy as a result of over-leveraged casino and hotel properties in Atlantic City.

## 2010–2012

DT flirts with the possibility of running for president, raising the "birther" issue concerning Barack Obama, which draws a lot of media attention. He decides against running—for now.

## 2015

DT formally announces his presidential bid for the 2016 election at Trump Tower (June 16). "I am officially running for president of the United States."

# Trump Online

For more information about Donald J. Trump, the following online resources are useful:

1. *www.donaldjtrump.com*, a political site that exclusively serves Trump's bid for the presidency, with updated news, position papers, and a store with merchandise (baseball caps, bumper stickers, T-shirts, etc.) themed "Make America Great Again!"
2. *www.trump.com*, a business site that exclusively serves his business interests, highlights the Trump Organization and all its assets/ventures.
3. *www.facebook.com/DonaldTrump*. "This is the official Facebook page for Donald J. Trump." It has 4,228,453 "likes" as of November 14, 2015.
4. *https://twitter.com/realDonaldTrump*. "The official Twitter profile for Donald Trump."
5. *www.youtube.com/DonaldTrump*. "The official YouTube channel for Donald Trump."
6. *www.nytimes.com*, the website for the *New York Times*, the hometown newspaper, and the best single source of information about Trump.
7. *www.PolitiFact.com* is a division of the *Tampa Bay Times*. From the website: "PolitiFact is an independent fact-checking journalism

website aimed at bringing you the truth in politics. PolitiFact's reporters and editors fact-check statements from the White House, Congress, candidates, advocacy groups and more, rating claims for accuracy on our Truth-O-Meter. Every fact-check includes analysis of the claim, an explanation of our reasoning and a list of links to all our sources."

*Note:* Trump proactively buys websites, to lock in key names—notably *www.donaldjtrump.com* and *www.trump.com.* "Trump's son, Eric, who is executive vice president of development and acquisitions at the Trump Organization, said the company acquires 'thousands' of domains each year. Eric Trump described the practice as 'business as usual' for the company. He said the more than 3,000 domains registered through the general counsel's e-mail address are just a fraction of the 'tens of thousands' of URLs owned by the company.'" ("Donald Trump owns thousands of secret web addresses," by Hunter Walker, BusinessInsider.com, August 13, 2015.)

# Trump Tomes

*Note: The books, arranged in order of publication date, include books he has published, and a book by his daughter Ivanka.*

*Trump: The Art of the Deal*, with Tony Schwartz (Random House, 1987).

His first bestseller, which he mentioned by name at Trump Tower when he announced his candidacy. The book begins with a chapter titled "A Week in the Life," a behind-the-scenes glimpse behind the curtain at what goes on at Trump Tower. (His office is on the twenty-sixth floor; his personal residence is in its top three floors.)

Bookended by "A Week in the Life" and "The Week That Was: How the Deals Came Out," the bulk of the book reinforces Trump's occupation—and preoccupation: "I like making deals, preferably big deals. That's how I get my kicks," he writes.

The book serves up biographical information to set the stage, but its main focus, as the title clearly states, is on his deal-making. Each major property has its own chapter, explaining how he went from the initial acquisition and beyond.

Principally inspirational reading for business types, the book comes full circle as Trump writes: "In my life, there are two things I've found I'm very good at: overcoming obstacles and motivating good people to do their best work . . . I also plan to keep making deals, big deals, and right around the clock."

In an introduction to *Trump: How to Get Rich* (2004), he wrote that it "became the bestselling business book of the decade, with over three million copies in print."

*Trump: Surviving at the Top*, with Charles Leerhsen (Random House, 1990).

Coming on the heels of Trump's first book, his second book had a lot to live up to. He felt "this second book should not simply continue the story of my major deals but should be a more personal work. I've scored some of the biggest victories of my career since my first book, but I've also faced some obstacles that taught me not to take the winning for granted. That's why I decided to call this book *Surviving at the Top*."

In the book's epigram, Trump quotes President Theodore Roosevelt's oft-quoted statement about credit given where it's due—to the one "who actually strives to do the deeds," and not his critics. It's obviously how Trump sees himself, and it's instrumental to his survival at the top.

In subject matter and treatment, this book recalls *Trump: The Art of the Deal*, since it discusses specific projects by chapter. (Why mess with a winning formula?)

The book ends with an illuminating chapter, "On Toughness," which is a Trump main trait. Even his critics will agree, perhaps anonymously and begrudgingly, that Trump's steely demeanor has served him well over the years. In this chapter, he writes: "I have a reputation for being tough, and I'd like to think it's justified. You must be tough when a lot of influential people are saying that your day has come and gone, when your marriage is breaking up, and when business pressures are increasing. Toughness, in the long run, is a major secret of my survival."

For anyone who read, and enjoyed, *Trump: The Art of the Deal*, this book will not disappoint: It's a second dip in the pool of hard-earned wisdom that comes from deal-making and deal-breaking at the Trump Organization.

*Trump: The Art of the Comeback*, with Kate Bohner (Times Books, 1997).

Like Steve Jobs—who engineered one of the most successful comebacks in American business when he returned to Apple—Trump has been there and done that. In fact, the title of this book is appropriately reflective and justifiably so.

In his introduction, he explains: "The banks were crawling all over me. The Gulf War had a disastrous effect on tourism. Cash flows were dwindling at my casinos. Then I missed a mortgage payment on the Castle in Atlantic City. All hell broke loose. Wall Street went nuts. The newspapers screamed of my demise. I was up against the wall.

"Then, one day around Christmas of 1990, I said to myself, Donald, it's time to fight back. So I got down to work. Today I'm over $3 billion in the black, I've paid off my personal debt, business is great . . ."

*Guinness World Records* credits him for the biggest financial turnaround in business history.

*The America We Deserve* (Renaissance Books: St. Martin's Press, 2000).

In the introduction ("The Serious Side of Trump"), he lays out exactly what this book is about: His growing dissatisfaction with our political system teeming with incompetent politicians who maintain the status quo at the public's expense. Foreshadowing his 2015 presidential bid, this book, published in 2000, lays out his reasons: "I will run if I become convinced I can win. Two things are certain at this point, however: I believe nonpoliticians represent the wave of the future and if elected I would make the kind of president America needs in the new millennium."

Eerily prescient, Trump's perception that nonpoliticians—and not career politicians—will come into their own, that their time has come, this book provides much food for thought, and provides insights into how Trump thinks and feels about our broken-down political system that is failing American voters.

*The Way to the Top: The Best Business Advice I Ever Received* (Random House, 2004).

This is a curated collection of original business advice that Trump solicited. His thesis: "there's simply no way to acquire all the wisdom you need to make your business thrive." His solution: "So I asked the brightest, most successful businessmen and women I know—and some I don't know—what was the best business advice they have ever received."

One sample: from Adam M. Aron (chairman and CEO of Vail Resorts, Inc.), "As much as possible, deal only with good and honorable people. If you deal with good people, you won't need a contract, and if you are dealing with bad people, no contract can protect you."

*Trump: How to Get Rich*, with Meredith McIver (Random House, 2004).

"*How to Get Rich*. That's what I decided to call it, because whenever I meet people, that's usually what they want to know from me. You ask a baker how he makes bread. You ask a billionaire how to makes money . . . Billionaire authors are harder to find."

A book of general business advice that explains Trump's mindset and values, which he considers essential to becoming not only rich, but Richie Rich rich (a Harvey comic book).

*Think Like a Billionaire: Everything You Need to Know About Success, Real Estate, and Life*, with Meredith McIver (Random House, 2004).

In his introduction, Trump explains that this should be considered part two of his previous book, *How to Get Rich* (2004). To my mind, this book should have more fully developed its principal theme, explaining how he went from being an apprentice in the family business, to become a millionaire, and then a billionaire.

In other words, instead of discussing billionaires as a group, which he does briefly in the introduction, he should more fully explain their mindset, and then show how they translate their thinking into businesses that proved profitable, how they managed their companies, and then discussed his own business in casebook fashion.

What were the thinking processes that led Bill Gates from writing computer code to helming Microsoft? Or Mark Zuckerberg from compiling Harvard's various "houses" into a social networking website that eventually encompassed the world? Or Steve Jobs, who sold Wozniak's hand-made computer and used his marketing genius to promote a user-friendly personal computer?

In Trump's case, what's the step-by-step plan that made him a multibillionaire? Inquiring minds want to know.

In this book, there's the obligatory "days in a week" chapter and a long chapter on "Inside *The Apprentice*," his reality television show. Both, however, would have been best reserved for other books, to give this one more focus.

Though there's a lot of information in the book, it should have simply been titled, *Donald Trump on Success in Life and Business.*

*Trump 101: The Way to Success*, with Meredith McIver (Wiley, 2006).

As the title suggests, this is a book of basic business wisdom, appropriate for someone new to business, and learning the ropes. In the introduction, Trump writes: "It is a collection of my beliefs about business and life—my basic rules and principles." Many of the themes he talks about in interviews can be found in this book: the importance of passion, insisting on perfection, setting the bar high—all familiar but time-tested advice.

*Why We Want You to be Rich: Two Men—One Message*, by Trump with Meredith McIver, and Robert Kiyosaki with Sharon Lechter (Rich Press, 2006).

When a millionaire meets a billionaire, this book is the result. Set in two different typefaces so you can easily distinguish between Trump's words and Kiyosaki's, this book's thesis is that financial education is what makes the difference between being poor or rich. From the introduction: "Their concern is that the rich are getting richer but America is getting poorer. Like the polar ice caps, the middle class is disappearing. America is becoming a two-class society. Soon you will be either rich or poor. Donald and Robert want you to be rich . . . Most people in the middle class are passive investors—investors who work and invest not to lose. The rich are active investors who work and invest to win. This book is about becoming . . . active investors—expanding your means to live a great life by working and investing to win."

With self-help quizzes, numerous graphics, and sidebars/quotes, this self-help book offers a lot of food for thought.

*Trump: Think Big and Kick Ass in Business and Life*, with Bill Zanker (HarperCollins, 2007).

Who is Bill Zanker, and why is he collaborating with Trump on a book? He's the guy who, in 1980, bootstrapped a $5,000 investment to start the Learning Annex, an adult education company. The classes are not academic in nature, but practical and popular. For example, classes include "How to Buy Foreclosed Property," and also "How to Make Your Own Soap."

In the introduction, Zanker writes: "Read each chapter, and let the Trump attitude sink in and teach you a lesson. Adapt Trump's bold, kick-ass attitude to fit your life. Use the Trump attitude to inspire you to break through the limits you have set for yourself."

Zanker's prescription: Inoculate yourself against the fear of failure by taking a healthy vitamin dose of Trump-tude.

In previous books, Trump provides specific information about the acquisition of properties; in this one, he talks tactics.

This is good, meaty information, and anyone who wants to explore Trump's mindset in dealing with others will get a full meal here.

*Trump: Never Give Up: How I Turned My Biggest Challenges Into Success*, with Meredith McIver (Wiley, 2008).

Appropriately, the first chapter focuses on a black swan event when two major, well-respected newspapers in New York—the *Wall Street Journal* and the *New York Times*—dumped on Trump in March 1991, "detailing my predicament and the total financial run that would happen at any moment . . . That was the lowest moment I had yet encountered in my life. The phones in my office were even quiet, which had never happened before."

After some soul-searching, Trump admitted he had "lost my perspective" and "had become complacent. My momentum wasn't where it should have been."

The situation: Trump had secured billions in loans and had "personally guaranteed $975 million of that debt. I could easily have gone bankrupt."

But Trump never gave up; he recovered from imminent financial disaster, and went on to succeed when others predicted certain failure for him. They were wrong, he was right.

Unlike his first book, *Trump: The Art of the Deal*, this book highlights lessons learned, drawn from specific building projects and situations. "As I went along," he writes, "I realized that every project came with its own set of major challenges, and I began to learn to expect them. That was okay because I was prepared. That's another reason I'm writing *Never Give Up*—to let you know you should be prepared and to try to help you with the situations you might encounter." Principally, Trump hammers home the point that if you want to be successful in life and business, you must learn to say no to "No." Don't let other people convince you that problems are insurmountable. As he explained in *Never Give Up*, "Why? Because when I hear the word 'No' it becomes a challenge to me. I believe the so-called impossible is actually very often possible, if you're willing to work very hard, and if you realize that problems can become opportunities."

*Trump-Style Negotiation: Powerful Strategies and Tactics for Mastering Every Deal*, by George H. Ross (Wiley, 2008).

If the author's name doesn't ring a bell, his employer surely does—Donald Trump. But chances are good that if you're a fan of *The Apprentice*, you've seen him on TV: He's a lawyer (senior counsel) for the Trump Organization, and also teaches courses on negotiation at New York University. In other words, he's a master negotiator and, as such, has much to share on the fine art of the deal.

A practical book jam-packed with advice, this book offers specific strategies on getting, and keeping, the upper hand, having a mindset geared toward effective negotiating, and highlighting the necessary people skills involved.

*Think Like a Champion: An Informal Education in Business and Life*, with Meredith McIver (Vanguard Press, 2009).

As Trump points out in the "introduction," people are always asking him for his "secrets" to success, as if a laundry list, if sedulously followed, will guarantee fame, fortune, and financial success!

It ain't *that* easy, as Trump himself will point out.

In this book, Trump explicates his "thought process that I believe can lead people to success . . . It's another side to my personality—the more reflective side that reveals my sources and how I apply them to the big picture that is life." His methodology: "I take a topic, think about it, dissect it, and put it back into a formula that becomes what I believe is solid advice."

This is a collection of informal essays on randomly arranged topics offering general advice on personal and business matters. A book of general wisdom, of lessons learned, is of particular interest to readers who don't want to know the case histories of all of Trump's deals, by property; instead, he examines specific attributes and working philosophies that, when taken together, will lead the reader to success. As such, it's for the lay reader and not just the business community.

*The Trump Card: Playing to Win in Work and Life*, by Ivanka Trump
(Touchstone, 2009).

Of Trump's three adult children from his first marriage, only one (so far) has
published a book: Ivanka Trump, who was twenty-seven years old when she
penned *The Trump Card*. In her introduction, "Get Over It," she explains,
"When I reach for a book to help me past a hurdle or two in my business life,
I don't go looking for a dry manual written by some sixty-year-old male,
reflecting on a long career." She instead looks for a book written by someone
her age, to whom she can relate.

Like her father and older brother, she graduated from the Wharton School
of Finance. Currently an executive vice-president of development and acquisitions of the Trump Organization, and one of the next generation that will
inherit and run the family business, Ivanka recently took center stage when
she introduced her dad at Trump Tower when he announced his candidacy for
the presidency.

This book, then, is ideally suited for twenty-somethings looking to make
their mark in the world, the ones starting out who, like herself, came into the
business world to find her or his place in it. (She points out that, yes, she's
had a lot of advantages, including working in the family business, but if she
couldn't cut it, she'd be fired. The door was open and an opportunity was
offered, but it was still up to her to earn it.)

*Time to Get Tough: Making America #1 Again* (Regnery Publishing, Inc., 2011).

A stark departure from his business-themed books, this is Trump's prescription on why and how America as a country needs to take names and kick ass;
in other words, it's time for America to stop being the punching bag and go on

the offensive to become, once again, the heavyweight champion of the world, instead of a lightweight.

The underlying theme is that the business of America is business, but that business has been undermined by indifferent and inept politicians and pussy-footing presidents that refuse to take a hard stance against the economic ills that afflict our country.

This is the original blueprint for Trump's 2006 run for the presidency, and as such, bears careful reading for anyone who wants to know what he thinks on the major issues—in short, his political platform and his prescription to cure our nation's ills.

In August 2015, on *www.donaldjtrump.com*, Trump began posting his position papers on major issues. For those who want a quick overview, this is his broad plan. Of particular interest: the book's afterword, in which he lays out his rationale for running for public office. In it, we learn that his third wife, Melania, told him: "Donald, people love you, but they wouldn't vote for you for president." He, of course, asked her why, and she explained, "You're a little wild and a little too controversial. They respect you, they think you're really smart—the smartest of all—but enough people just wouldn't vote for you."

As time went on, Melania changed her mind, and urged him to run because "now you could win, and maybe even easily. People really want you. I see it on the streets. People want you and they really need you."

That, I think, was the tipping point. Trump then decided it warranted serious thought and wrote: "My primary reason for running for presidency would be to straighten out the mess Obama has made of our country . . . And whether it's me or someone else, we need the kind of thinking that can produce this kind of success," referring to his success as the head of the Trump Organization.

The book concludes: "But we need smart leaders, people who understand how the world works and have the guts to get tough. With proper leadership, we can rebuild the shining city on a hill we once were. When we do, we should boldly and proudly celebrate America's power and dominance in the world . . . If we do that, we can, together, make America #1 again."

Four years later, Trump decided it was finally time to get serious, and announce his candidacy for the presidency.

Note: The first chapter of the paperback edition (2015) has been updated to reflect recent events.

*Midas Touch: Why Some Entrepreneurs Get Rich—And Why Most Don't*, by Donald J. Trump and Robert Kiyosaki (Plata Publishing, 2011).

The Midas Touch hand is the ideal metaphor to represent the attributes critical to entrepreneurial success. The attributes are: strength of character, focus, brand, relationships, and the little things. Taken together, "when all the awareness, skill, learning, and knowledge are in your hands, that's when the true Midas Touch power really shines."

Recognizing that governments and schools don't create jobs, that only entrepreneurs do, this book lays out their prescription on "what it takes to become a successful entrepreneur."

They encourage readers to develop entrepreneurial skills and take control of their financial lives by becoming risk-takers.

*Crippled America: How to Make America Great Again* (Threshold Editions, 2015).

Given that Trump is running for president, his views on what politically ails this country and his prescription for fixing them is a timely subject, though nothing new. He's been speaking and writing about this subject for years and now feels the tipping point has been reached. Unless drastic and immediate action is taken, our country faces default and insolvency because the national debt has grown to titanic proportions. We are, he asserts, looking over the edge of a financial abyss that will dwarf the economic collapse of 2007–2008. He also asserts that career politicians have proven themselves incapable and unwilling to make the fixes necessary. They aren't the solution, he believes, because they are part of the problem.

Trump's growing dissatisfaction with the American political system is in tune with many Americans who feel disenfranchised. He is writing to that target audience, who share his views that politics as usual isn't working now, and hasn't worked for some years. It's time to shake things up, and it's time for major changes by ousting career politicians and replacing them with non-politicians who will serve American voters in good stead.

# Coda

*"It is no longer inconceivable that Trump could win the GOP nomination—unlikely, but not inconceivable."*

—"Trump's singular 'platform,'" by Ruth Marcus,
*Washington Post*, August 26, 2015

When Donald J. Trump announced his candidacy on June 16, 2015, for the presidency, running on the Republican ticket, the catcalls began. The old-timers in the GOP scoffed, the media had a field day, the late night TV show comedians mined it for all it was worth, saying that all that glittered was not gold, and talking heads on TV weighed in with their collective wisdom, pontificating that Trump was not, as he is at the Trump Organization, the man who would be king—or, in this case, the next person to sit in the Oval Office in Washington, D.C., as the president of the United States.

But as former New Jersey governor and Republican Tom Kean Sr. was quoted in the *Washington Post* (August 21, 2015), in a story by Robert Costa and Philip Rucker, as saying, "Everyone underestimated him terribly from

Day One. But as someone who knows him and knew his father—the whole family—I can assure you, that was a mistake."

"No one," said Kean, "has figured out how to handle Trump."

Standing at the eye of a media storm, Trump is in the race for the long haul, to the dismay of his critics, of which there are many, and to the delight of his supporters, who are showing up in record numbers at his rallies to hear his message on how he plans to make America great again.

Trump, it seems, is everywhere, to the dismay of the other presidential candidates, regardless of political affiliation, who can't get a fraction of the attention from the media they so desperately need.

Trump, who in the past had made head fakes about running for high office, is not faking now; in fact, he's got the ball and he's driving toward the basket, aiming for a slam dunk. It's now time for him to make his move: He will be seventy years old on June 14, 2016, and if he fails to win the party's nomination as the candidate of choice for the 2016 election, he is not likely to run again.

This is it. It's show time, and nobody can put on a bigger, better, and louder show than Donald Trump. He is larger than life—in fact, to use one of his favorite words, *huge*. In the words of *Time* magazine, which once again put him on its cover for its August 24, 2015, issue, "The Donald Has Landed. Deal with it."

The photo shows Trump in his office at Trump Tower, wearing a business suit, and a leather glove on which is perched an American eagle.

His critics cry: Foul play! It's outrageous! It's grandstanding!

Trump doesn't care. He's taken the heat from his critics for over four decades. He can tough it out for his campaign to become the next president.

*Time* magazine's advice? "Deal with it."

# DEAL WITH IT

Though Trump's critics don't want to "deal with it"—in fact, they'd like to see him vacate the room, so to speak, because he's sucking all of the oxygen out of it—and they'd prefer to see a more traditional Republican candidate step to the forefront. Donald Trump's thrown his hat in the ring, and he's in for the long haul. He'll stay in the race as long as necessary to win, as long as he's got the poll numbers and the support from voters whom he's confident will rally behind him.

As of this writing, Trump's ahead in the polls by a significant margin, flummoxing his critics. As Robert Costa and Philip Rucker ("GOP field wrestles a Trump tornado," August 21, 2015) wrote in the *Washington Post*, "Donors feel powerless. Republican officials have little leverage. Candidates are skittish. Super PAC operatives say attack ads against him could backfire. And everyone agrees the Trump factor in this chaotic multi-candidate field is so unpredictable that any move carries dangerous risks."

Politics is, after all, risky business with high stakes. This time, the stakes can't be any higher: Trump sees doom and gloom looming on the horizon—unless someone, preferably himself, takes charge. His prescriptions: it's "time to get tough," it's time to "think big and kick ass," and it's time to negotiate from a position of strength with foreign countries by using "the art of the deal." We used to be a great country once upon a time, Trump says, and we need to rebound—it's time for "the art of the comeback," it's time to "think like a champion."

Trump has trumped the competition because, as *Time* magazine (August 24, 2015) pointed out in its cover story, "You need only listen to that message of disgust, for the political system, its falsehoods and failure, which has taken Trump to the top of the Republican polls."

Plain people want plain talk, and that's what Trump's delivering. It's tough talk, more from the heart than the head, and his messages appeal to a large body of disaffected people who have effectively said: We've given politicians many chances, and they've consistently failed. Our country's in one hell of a mess. We've forgotten the business of America is business, so why not try a successful businessman instead?

Take a good look at the *Time* magazine cover with its head shot of Trump. His eyes are steely; his thick brows are beetled; and he's not smiling—he's not scowling, but it's an expression that shows he's just had it with politicians in general: This is Trump's war face.

As *Time* reminds us: Deal with it.

*"Here's the bottom line: Any political leader who won't face the future head-on is putting the American Dream at risk. That dream has made this the best country in history. It's the dream my father and mother dreamed, the one they made come true for our family. It's the one that took me to the top."*

—Donald Trump, *The America We Deserve* (2000)

# Index

# About the Author

**GEORGE BEAHM** is a *New York Times* bestselling author who has published extensively on prominent business figures and also popular culture. A former U.S. Army officer who has served on active duty with the First Infantry Division, he later served in the Virginia Army National Guard, and in the Army Reserve. Beahm lives in southeast Virginia with his wife Mary, a teacher. His website: *www.GeorgeBeahm.com.*